Art and Design
Complete Revision and Practice

Keith Winser

Published by BBC Active, an imprint of Educational Publishers LLP, part of the Pearson Education Group Edinburgh Gate, Harlow, Essex CN20 2JE, England

ISBN 978-1-4066-5436-3

Printed in China CTPSC/01

The Publisher's policy is to use paper manufactured from sustainable forests.

First published 2005

This edition 2010

Minimum recommended system requirements
PC: Windows(r), XP sp2, Pentium 4 1 GHz processor (2 GHz for Vista), 512 MB of RAM (1 GB for Windows Vista), 1 GB of free hard disk space, CD-ROM drive 16x, 16 bit colour monitor set at 1024 x 768 pixels resolution
MAC: Mac OS X 10.3.9 or higher, G4 processor at 1 GHz or faster, 512 MB RAM, 1 GB free space (or 10% of drive capacity, whichever is higher), Microsoft Internet Explorer® 6.1 SP2 or Macintosh Safari™ 1.3, Adobe Flash® Player 9 or higher, Adobe Reader® 7 or higher, Headphones recommended

If you experiencing difficulty in launching the enclosed CD-ROM, or in accessing content, please review the following notes:
1 Ensure your computer meets the minimum requirements. Faster machines will improve performance.
2 If the CD does not automatically open, Windows users should open 'My Computer', double-click on the CD icon, then the file named 'launcher.exe'. Macintosh users should double-click on the CD icon, then 'launcher.osx'
Please note: the eDesktop Revision Planner is provided as-is and cannot be supported.
For other technical support, visit the following address for articles which may help resolve your issues:
http://centraal.uk.knowledgebox.com/kbase/

If you cannot find information which helps you to resolve your particular issue, please email: Digital.Support@pearson.com.
Please include the following information in your mail:
- Your name and daytime telephone number.
- ISBN of the product (found on the packaging.)
- Details of the problem you are experiencing - e.g. how to reproduce the problem, any error messages etc.
- Details of your computer (operating system, RAM, processor type and speed if known.)

Contents

Introduction   iv

About GCSE Art and Design   vi

The 5 Ps to GCSE success   viii

Studying Art and Design   x

Definitions of art, craft and design   xii

Topic checker   *

Your work journal

Using your work journal   2

Recording observations and ideas   4

Finding a context for your work   6

Experimenting with media   8

Improving your work   10

Mixed media and 3-D processes   12

Improving your visual research skills   14

Making good use of ICT   16

Connecting with other artists' work   18

Take up the SEMI approach   20

Worksheet   22

Using other artists' ideas   24

Art history pages

How to use the art history pages   26

Art from Africa   28

Art from the Americas   32

Art from Asia and the East   36

Oceanic art   40

European art, craft and design   44

Art, craft and design in the UK   48

Women artists and designers   52

Contemporary art, craft and design   56

Developing your ideas   60

Useful annotations   62

A critical vocabulary   64

Writing frames

The Assessment Objectives in student-friendly form 66
Assessment Objective 1 Writing Frame 1/1 67
Assessment Objective 1 Writing Frame 1/2 68
Assessment Objective 1 Writing Frame 1/3 69
Assessment Objective 2 Writing Frame 2/1 70
Assessment Objective 2 Writing Frame 2/2 71
Assessment Objective 3 Writing Frame 3/1 72
Assessment Objective 3 Writing Frame 3/2 73
Assessment Objective 4 Writing Frame 4/1 74
Assessment Objective 4 Writing Frame 4/2 75

GCSE exam

Starting points 76
The exam days 78
Planning for your exam writing frame 80
Exam-day essentials 82
Achieving a high-quality outcome 83
When the exam is over 84
Self-assessment questions 85
Saying 'why' and not just 'what' 86
Student checklist 88
Displaying your work 89

Glossaries and word banks 90

Web links *

Acknowledgements 100

* Only available in the CD-ROM version of the book.

Introduction

How to use GCSE Bitesize Complete Revision and Practice

Begin with the CD-ROM. There are five easy steps to using the CD-ROM – and to creating your own personal revision programme. Follow these steps and you'll be fully prepared for the exam without wasting time on areas you already know.

Topic checker

Step 1: Check

The Topic checker will help you figure out what you know – and what you need to revise.

Revision planner

Step 2: Plan

When you know which topics you need to revise, enter them into the handy Revision planner. You'll get a daily reminder to make sure you're on track.

Step 3: Revise

From the Topic checker, you can go straight to the topic pages that contain all the facts you need to know.

- Give yourself the edge with the Web*Bite* buttons. These link directly to the relevant section on the BBC Bitesize Revision website.

- Audio*Bite* buttons let you listen to more about the topic to boost your knowledge even further. *

Step 4: Practise

Check your understanding by answering the Practice questions. Click on each question to see the correct answer.

Exam Bite

Step 5: Exam

Are you ready for the exam? Exam*Bite* buttons take you to an exam question on the topics you've just revised. *

* Not all subjects contain these features, depending on their exam requirements.

About this book

This book is your all-in-one companion for GCSE Art and Design. As with all Bitesize guides it is intended to help with revision for your GCSE examination. In art and design this guide will help you improve your chances of success with coursework as well as your terminal examination. It is about the processes you need to adopt to be successful throughout the course as well as the quality of the final products you create.

This Bitesize book is divided into five sections:

'Your work journal' is about developing good habits when using your sketchbook or 'work journal' as we shall call it. How you use this is crucial to achieving success in your GCSE, and it is something you should consider right from the start of the course. Indeed, if you wait until your exam before you use your work journal properly, you're almost too late!

The **art history pages** are designed to help you make links between your work and that of other artists, craftworkers and designers from a range of countries and historical periods. This section contains easy-to-use charts, examples, and tips to help you use the chart to develop your own work and a critical vocabulary.

Tree **(after Gilbert and George) – acrylic on canvas**

Mural panel design for travel agent – acrylic on panel

The **writing frames** will help you to think critically and write critically about your work. You can photocopy these pages, fill them in and paste them into your work journal.

The section on the **GCSE exam** guides you through the exam period from start to finish. It explains how to prepare for the exam and to use the preparation period to best effect. You are shown how to find good starting points for your work and how to develop your ideas. It also tells you about the exam days and explains how to plan your work to make the most of the two five-hour periods. For many students, producing a piece of artwork in this time is one of the most worrying parts of GCSE Art and Design. Being properly prepared and organised is crucial.

This section also offers help and advice about what to do after the exam is over, including evaluating your work and displaying it in ways that present it in the best light.

First-hand observation in pencil – study of a bicycle

At the end of the book there is a reference section with **glossaries and word banks** of terms used in art, craft and design. You should become familiar with them and use them alongside your practical work.

About GCSE Art and Design

> GCSE Art and Design is made up of two parts which, when added together, give you your GCSE grade.

> There are four assessment objectives and it is very important that you show how well you can work in ALL FOUR areas.

Art and design components

remember >>

What you do is for your teachers to mark – you don't need to tell them what they already know!

GCSE Art and Design is made up of two parts or 'components'. These are marked separately and the marks added together to give you your GCSE grade. The two components are **controlled assessment** (this used to be the coursework part, but is now a portfolio – a more limited selection of work) and an **externally set assignment (ESA)** or task set by examiners – not your teachers – that comes at the end of the whole course.

- Controlled assessment marks make up 60 per cent of your final total and the externally set task makes up the other 40 per cent.
- The work you do for the controlled assessment component will be supervised by your art teacher to make sure that it is completely your own.
- You will also have some responsibility for selecting samples from this component for marking either towards the end of Year 10, or near the end of the course in Year 11.
- Although this book makes reference to **examiners**, your teachers in school will mark all of your coursework and the ESA.
- So actually it is your teachers who are the examiners – they have to mark your work, assessing it against the **assessment objectives**.
- The marks they give will be checked by a representative from the awarding body, called a moderator.
- Moderators are trained in assessing work to GCSE standards and they have the responsibility to make sure that your teacher's marks are accurate and match current standards.

Mural panels for car showroom, two students working together to produce a joint mural for their ESA

Different forms of GCSE Art and Design

GCSE Art and Design is available in a number of different forms. The most common GCSE Art and Design course is called **Unendorsed**.

- Unendorsed is a general art, craft and design course where you experience a range of different activities.

Awarding bodies (the organisations that used to be called exam boards) also offer **Endorsed GCSEs**.

- Endorsed GCSEs are options where you specialise in a certain type of art, craft or design.
- You could specialise in, for example, fine art, graphic design, textiles, film and photography, three-dimensional design or even critical studies (an option where you can write about art as much as make art yourself!)

Awarding bodies also offer **Short Course GCSEs** and **Applied GCSEs**.

- Short course GCSEs are worth half a full GCSE because you only produce half the work – apart from this difference everything else is the same.

- Applied GCSEs are worth two GCSEs because you produce twice the amount of work, but they are also designed differently and include project briefs and activities that imitate art and design in the commercial world. This GCSE course is good for students who have already decided that they want a career in the art, craft or design industry.

This range of options can be confusing – for teachers let alone students! If your school has different options available, talk to your art teachers to agree which one is best for you.

study hint >>

It is possible to take GCSE Art and Design and GCSE Applied Art and Design.

GCSE Art and Design assessment objectives

Despite all these differences, all GCSE Art and Design courses have the same **four assessment objectives (AOs)**. Every awarding body has to use the same basic format laid down by the Qualifications and Curriculum Authority (QCA), which is a government body. This means that wherever you do GCSE in England and Wales you will be tested on the same things and to the same standard.

The AOs in full are:

AO1 develop ideas through investigations informed by contextual and other sources, demonstrating analytical and cultural understanding;

AO2 refine ideas through experimenting and selecting appropriate resources, media, materials, techniques and processes;

AO3 record ideas, observations and insights relevant to intentions in visual and/or other forms;

AO4 present a personal, informed and meaningful response demonstrating analytical and critical understanding, realising intentions and, where appropriate, making connections between visual, written, oral and other elements.

To anyone other than an examiner these descriptions can seem pretty meaningless – as you go through this book we put the AOs into a more easily understood form and explain just what you have to do to meet them.

But it is important that you understand just what your work **is** going to be marked on – you don't want to spend too much of the limited time available producing work that will not gain you the precious marks needed to achieve the grade you deserve!

You must try to make sure that you show the highest level you can achieve in **each** of the different assessment objectives. It is not unusual for students to achieve more highly in some areas and less so in others – after all most of us are better at some things than others and the assessment will show this – but it is best to be as consistent as possible.

>> key fact Don't ignore any parts of the AOs: if you miss out on some areas, your marks – and therefore your final GCSE grade – will be affected.

The 5 Ps to GCSE success

 Follow the 5 Ps to exam success:
Planning
Process
Purpose
Practice
Product.

Planning

>> **key fact** **Students who get the best grades are those who plan what they do carefully and don't leave everything to the last minute or, worse still, just hope that it'll be all right in the end.**

If you get the chance to watch artists or designers at work, it sometimes looks like they are 'making it up as they go along', or that they are just doing what they feel like doing whenever they like. But, more often than not, what they are doing is **meticulously planned** and **organised in advance**. It may be in their heads, and it is often a result of several years of experimenting and practice, but planned it is. Planning is crucial to success in your GCSE.

Process

Every single thing you do as you work is an important part of the process of making your work better. Making mistakes is the best way of demonstrating this.

>> **key fact** **When things go 'wrong', you have a chance to show the examiner how you can learn to improve your work and make it better.**

- Take time out to ask yourself exactly what's wrong.
- Why did it go wrong?
- Make a note of your thoughts on the paper.
- Have another go!

Developing a positive attitude to mistakes is very important. It is through making mistakes that we learn how to improve. In fact, making mistakes is essential, because it gives you a chance to show that you can do something better!

**Bicycle study,
paint and pencil**

Celebrity, **ideas development
collage, work journal pages**

Purpose

Having a purpose for your work is very important. **Keep in mind the question, 'Why am I doing this?' and try to answer it on the pages of your work journal.**

- A few **written notes**, or **annotations**, explaining what's going through your head are all that is needed here.
- You do not need to write a lot in GCSE Art and Design.
- Art and design examiners much prefer looking at pictures to reading huge amounts of text.
- At all times it's better to explain in visual form rather than in words, but adding a few notes to explain why you did something can be helpful and informative to the examiner.

Practice

Everyone has heard the phrase **'practice makes perfect'**, and this is as true in art and design as in any other walk of life. The trouble is, even the best art and design students sometimes forget it.

- It is very important to develop and practise your art skills.
- Practice, whether drawing the same object from different angles or using a specific art material to try to achieve different effects, is essential to GCSE success.
- If you don't practise, you will not be in control of the materials you use: they will 'control' you, allowing it to be a matter of luck whether your work is a success or not.

> **study hint >>**
> The more you practise, the more power you have. Practice means power!

> **study hint >>**
> Think like a snooker player: 'Am I able to control where the balls go, or do they go where they want?'

Product

What is the product of art, craft and design? In short, it is the end result of whatever the artist intended, be it a drawing, painting, sculpture, mixed-media or textile construction, a print or a photograph.

- All products have one thing in common: 'quality'.
- No self-respecting professional artist, craftworker or designer was ever happy with anything that was not the very best quality – and so it must be with you and your GCSE artwork.
- The 'quality' of an artwork can be seen in the materials from which it's made, the skill or craft that went into making it and the way it's presented.
- Use the three headings of **'material'**, **'skill'**, **'display'**, and ask yourself if your product is the best quality you can produce.

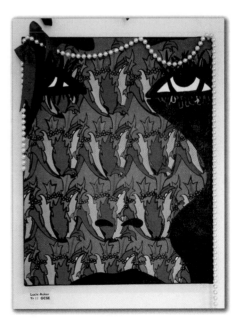

Icon, paint on canvas

Studying art and design

 Being skilful is not enough; you have to know about art as well.

 How well you understand what you do is almost as important as how well you can do it.

Widen your knowledge

The wide world of art, craft and design is so big it's almost impossible to imagine.

- It includes everything that any artist, craftworker and designer has ever created since the beginning of time to the present day, in any part of the world and for any useful or decorative purpose. It's no small challenge to know even where to begin!
- GCSE Art and Design is called a **'non-content specific'** subject.
- This means that, unlike history, for example, it is not laid down exactly which artists, styles of art, types of design or craft activities you should learn about.
- In this way, revising for art and design is unlike other subjects where you can be tested on your knowledge with practice questions.
- You do have to show how knowledgeable you are about art, craft and design to be successful at GCSE. One advantage with art and design (among many) is that you are free to choose the aspects of the subject that interest you. Successful students make the most of this freedom.

> **study hint >>**
>
> **Look beyond your own cultural background to find styles and types of art, craft and design that appeal to you.**

Deepen your understanding

> **study hint >>**
>
> **Use the notes and annotations you make in your work journal to show how well you understand what to do.**

>> key fact How well you think about what you do in art and design is very important for success at GCSE.

- It's a common view that art, craft and design is just about 'doing'.
- Of course, it is basically a practical subject, one where you 'get your hands dirty' and one where you use tools, materials and special equipment to create images and objects.
- But, it also needs thinking about. The more you understand about what you do, the more effective and successful your outcomes will be.

>> key fact Some choices are instinctive, but others need to be thought through to get the best effect.

Cave Art, collage

Practise your skills

'I can't draw' is heard all too often in schools and even amongst GCSE Art and Design students. What they really mean is, 'I'm having problems trying to draw something and make it look like I want it to'. Everyone experiences this from time to time, and how you deal with it says a lot about you.

- How good are you at taking on something new and practising it until you're good at it? A sport, for example, or learning to play a musical instrument?
- As we have already seen, art, craft and design is a practical subject. It is no coincidence that the words **'practical'** and **'practice'** have the same origin. **In order to be practical you must practise!**
- A major problem in art and design is caused by the idea of 'talent'. Artists are often described as 'talented', as though this is something they are born with! Many people have studied this and have tried to prove whether it is true. There is a lot less truth in it than commonly thought.

>> key fact Art, craft and design skills can be taught and learnt, and your own artistic capability can be improved by practice and experience.

Smiley (after Warhol), acrylic

Being an artist versus being a GCSE student

What are the differences and similarities between being an artist in your own right and being a GCSE student in a school?

- Both artists and students use art, craft or design materials and processes.
- Both gain inspiration from work that has gone before.
- Both create finished pieces of work for public display.
- Professional artists, craftworkers and designers don't have examiners checking up on their work – you do!

Remember, a student is a person who studies, but an artist, craftworker or designer produces art, craft or design work in their own right.

GCSE Art and Design is a course of study of art, craft and design. The course should help you to understand how artists and designers 'tick'. Hold on to the idea that you are **learning by doing**, and this will help you to keep things in perspective.

Definitions of art, craft and design

- Look for the differences between artists, craftworkers and designers.

- Find out why artists, craftworkers and designers do what they do.

Defining your activity

Not everybody is clear about the differences between art, craft and design. Often it doesn't really matter what you are doing is called: if the purpose of the activity is clear, it can often decide for you!

>> key fact It may help you to understand the differences between art, craft and design if you imagine the professional equivalent of what you are planning to do.

- If what you are doing would normally be done by an artist (for example, a painter or sculptor), it is probably art.
- If you think the activity would be done by a craftworker (for example, a potter or weaver), it is probably craft.
- If you are planning to decorate your bedroom, like an interior designer, or to print lengths of paper or fabric, like a surface pattern and textiles designer, the activity is design.

Art is ... what artists do

In the Western 'fine art' tradition, artists draw, paint and make sculptures using subjects that fall into the three categories of:

- **still life** (objects)
- **portraits** (human forms in general)
- **landscape** (scenes of the natural or built environment).

In more recent times, artists have explored all sorts of ways to express themselves. They have:

- 'painted' with fire, steam, smoke and bodies smeared with paint
- made sculptures with earth, bricks, rotting flesh, preserved animals, leaves floating in streams
- used new technology and methods to express their ideas.

study hint >>

The most challenging art often creates more problems for the viewer than it solves.

>> key fact Whether traditional or not in their approach, all artists have one thing in common: a personal drive to create some form of visual response to ideas or emotions of immense personal, social or even global significance.

Crafts are the activities craftworkers do

Craftworkers are hands on, **materials orientated** practitioners. They create high-quality objects and images that demonstrate their level of practical skill, using techniques that range from the most traditional to the most up to date.

- Craftworkers develop creatively by inventing new and ever more demanding ways of using materials and processes.
- Often craft is seen as making 'useful' things, but much craftwork is decorative as well as functional.
- Many contemporary craftworks are so highly designed or crafted that they are works of art in their own right – whether or not they are actually used for anything.

In any type of craft, people have different levels of expertise and status, for example, from a potter working from home, making and selling well-crafted household items to a Turner Prize-winning ceramicist making and exhibiting sculptural forms in porcelain for the international art market.

Design is a process, but also an occupation

>> **key fact** **All artists and craftworkers use design processes as they work.**

- Activities such as playing with different ideas, making choices, problem-solving, changing, improving and evaluating take place during most practical work.
- The period between starting out with an idea and presenting the final artistic outcome is essentially the **design process**.
- More recently, the idea of Design (with a capital 'D') has become an end in itself and now has a place alongside art and craft. The design industry is a powerful economic force in the country, and designers educated in Britain are highly sought after worldwide.

A measure of good quality design is where the look of something and how well it does its job works in perfect harmony. An artist might create a crazy building that is imaginative, fascinating and wild – but likely to fall down. A technically minded building engineer might make a strong and sturdy building that is boring to look at and oppressive to live or work in. A good architect, however, using their design skills, can create a quality building that is as good to look at as it is practical and sound.

The artist is not a special kind of man, but every man is a special kind of artist.
Ananda Coomraswamy

He who works with his hands is a labourer. He who works with his hands and his head is a craftsman. He who works with his hands, his head and his heart is an artist.
St Francis of Assisi

Using your work journal

- Get into the habit of calling your sketchbook your 'work journal'.
- Choose the right size and shape.
- Show your visual journey from start to finish.
- It's important to make mistakes!

What size and shape is right for you?

Work journals can fit into a back pocket or a back pack. An ideal approach is to have

- a tiny book for quick sketches, doodles, notes and ideas
- a larger (A3) spiral-bound hardback where you can develop and practise your skills and use a wide range of art materials and processes.

Your work journal needs to be tough and well bound – it will get a battering as you paste a range of work into it and carry it around. Fewer sheets of good quality heavyweight (120 gsm) **cartridge** paper is better than many sheets of thin paper.

Make your journal a work of art in itself. Take care to protect delicate work:

- Fix **charcoal drawings** with **fixative** or hairspray.
- Cover **chalk**, **pastel** or **charcoal** drawings with tracing or tissue paper.
- Use glue carefully to avoid pages sticking together. They might get torn when separated.

> **study hint >>**
> Put a sheet of card under the page when working to protect the work on the other side.

> *Success is going from failure to failure without losing enthusiasm.*
> **Winston Churchill**

> **study hint >>**
> Change the surface of every other sheet in your journal with different papers: anaglyptic wallpaper, tissue paper, brown wrapping paper and so on. Work on top of these new surfaces.

A good work journal reflects your personality

Going on a visual journey ...

- Use your journal, every day if you can, to record things you see and ideas that pop into your head.
- You may not see the relevance of everything you gather at first, but keep it anyway. It is important to show how you can use some things but not others from what you collect.
- Include brief notes beside the work to explain your **train of thought**.
- Write the date when you did the work and, if relevant, how long it took.
- Show your journal to another student or an adult and see if they can follow the 'journey'.

Think of your visual journey as a sightseeing tour where you travel around slowly, sometimes doubling back on yourself. The start and finish points might not be interesting or even far away from each other, but it is the journey that is exciting, enjoyable and memorable!

What to put in and what to leave out

It is possible to cover virtually all of the assessment objectives for GCSE in your work journal:

- your first ideas for a new topic
- your research into famous and not-so-famous artists and designers
- drawings and paintings, sketches, plans and designs.

Glue a copy of the **GCSE assessment objectives** onto the first page of your journal.

- Keep checking back to make sure you are on track.
- You can decorate this page with your name or nickname, or with patterns and drawings that remind you of what the assessment objectives mean.

To be successful, the work in your work journal must be **original**, and created and completed by you. Only copy other artists' work if you can include a note explaining what you have learnt by doing it.

Artist research (Gerald Scarfe), pen and ink, work journal page

Barriers (idea development), work journal pages

Anyone who never made a mistake has never tried anything new.
Albert Einstein

Recording observations and ideas

Working from first-hand observation

This art process is given many different names: **primary research**, **objective drawing** and **first-hand observation**.

- It means producing studies (usually drawings) from looking at real things in front of you.
- In its most 'traditional' form, objects are arranged as a display – a **still life** – so that you can look carefully at the spaces between the different objects and at the background as well as at the objects themselves.
- Don't avoid practising your observation drawing skills.
- Whatever theme you are working on, you must include some drawn studies of some real objects.
- Artists take time to examine what they look at and observe objects in great detail, noticing tiny differences in the shape and form.

>> **key fact** Practising first-hand drawing trains you to use your eyes to observe, and it should not be underestimated just how important this is.

study hint >>

Copying from photographs is not first-hand observation, taking photographs is. Using a camera to record something is not the same skill as drawing it by hand.

Bicycle study, direct observation in pencil

Researching secondary sources

Secondary source material is anything you find and use in your work that was created by someone else. This form of research involves collecting images and objects that help you to shape and form your own ideas. Pictures photocopied from books, downloaded from the Internet (and printed out) or cut from magazines are typical.

- Simply collecting pictures doesn't take you far up the assessment objective scale. Just how difficult is it to get a lot of pictures together on a theme these days? One click on an **image search engine** such as **www.picsearch.co.uk** or **http://images.google.co.uk** and it's done for you.
- To get the highest grades you must show how your research fits in with your intention.
- Select material that is relevant to what you want to do in the end.
- Show the examiner how your research is leading you towards your **final outcome** by organising the work in a logical way. Tell the story of what you did and what you intend to do next.

>> **key fact** Remember, the **keys** to good research are **select** and **organise**.

Bicycle study merged with Hockney

Artist study (David Hockney)

Making the most of secondary sources

Examiners report that too many GCSE students seem to avoid first-hand observation in favour of secondary research, and that too much secondary research is made up from photocopies from art books easily available in school. It is important to make proper use of secondary sources, for example:

- Show that you have chosen examples that are relevant to your theme, and explain in notes why you have chosen them.
- Don't throw away the examples that are not needed: you might find them useful later.
- Explaining why you rejected something can be as telling as saying why you chose something else.
- Organise your collection to show the process of your research and how you intend to use what you have collected.

Examples of secondary sources

Photographs from magazines are the most common examples, but work by other artists is much better.

- It doesn't matter whether you can identify who created the work or not, although if you can you may be able to find more examples by the same person to add to your research.
- Art galleries, museums and artists' own websites provide good sources for research.

Useful websites

www.cubittartists.org.uk, contemporary art gallery

http://www.sculpture.org.uk, twentieth century British sculpture

www.artlex.com, dictionary of art terms

www.indiaart.com, art forms of India

www.si.edu, Smithsonian Institute

www.sculptureplace.com, contemporary sculpture

www.alifetimeofcolor.com/study/timeline.html, timeline of art from prehistory to today

www.ibiblio.org/wm/paint/tl, timeline of painting styles and painters

www.guggenheim.or, international contemporary art

www.metmuseum.org/toah, Metropolitan Museum of Art timeline of art

www.artinliverpool.com, galleries and artists in Liverpool

http://witcombe.sbc.edu/ARTHLinks.html, art history resources

www.artcyclopedia.com, fine art search engine

www.getty.edu, Getty Museum

www.tate.org.uk, Tate Galleries across the UK

http://www.africanart.org, website of African art

www.vam.ac.uk, Victoria and Albert Museum

www.graffiti.org, graffiti from all over the world

www.graffiticreator.net, graffiti art creator

www.vroosh.com/search/art.html, art website links – a good starting point

www.artchive.com, Mark Harden's art archive

www.wwar.com, World Wide Art Resources

www.deviantart.com, world-wide community of artists

Finding a context for your work

 The **context** is the setting for the work, which can explain its purpose, reason or intention.

 The best contexts for art and design study are real ones.

The context 'sets the scene'

The setting for a work of art, craft and design is called its **context**. This might be obvious and dramatic, or it might be hidden away so that you need to do some digging to discover it.

- Investigating the context of works of art, craft and design is a two-way process, it might inspire the work, or be influenced by it.
- A close study of the artwork can give you an insight into the artist's life and times, thoughts, ideas and opinions.

>>  **Does a work of art reflect the time in which it was created or does it help to shape the world around it?**

The environment

Are you concerned for the environment? Whether a **local issue** such as the siting of a supermarket or the building of a by-pass, or a **global issue** such as nuclear power or global warming, if you have views on the topics below, could you use them to inspire your artwork?

conservation	town planning	factory-farming
green issues	the green belt	acid rain
pollution	motorways/by-passes	sea levels
litter	airport expansion	genetically modified crops
vandalism	industrialisation	

Society and your community

What is happening in your local community? What opinions do you and your friends and family have about these issues?

one-parent families	anti-social behaviour	care in the community
family breakdown	the class system	crime
peer-group pressure	sexism	drugs
bullying	immigration	
racism		

True art takes note not merely of form but also of what lies behind.
Mahatma Gandhi

The economy

What do you know about the way money affects you, your life and your future? What do you think about that? Consider these issues for your work.

employment unemployment the art market mass production	'cost of everything – value of nothing' global trading privatisation the value of antiques	public and private ownership transport issues artists-in-residence projects

Politics

Politicians may make the laws, the rules we have to live by, but when we vote, we give the power to them to do this. What do you think about this? Here are some themes to inspire artwork that says something about your opinions.

political parties extremism money and power state systems	schools the NHS public services the police state	mass protest equality identity cards the 'Nanny State'

Sites of visual interest and inspiration

- animal sanctuaries, city farms, zoos, RSPB sanctuaries, RSPCA
- airport viewing platforms
- visitor-friendly army/air force bases
- landscaped gardens
- archaeological digs and heritage sites
- industrial or commercial areas, docks, fisher fleets
- architectural practices, newspaper offices
- film, TV, radio and recording studios

Places to find contexts

- galleries: local, regional and or national
- museums: local history, general or specialised
- artists' studios and workshops
- theatre, festivals, community arts events
- collections of fairground art and equipment
- agricultural ephemera
- transport museums and collections
- social history collections and museums
- town and country houses
- specialised private collections
- fabrics, textiles and costumes

study hint >>

Check out the Tourist Information Centre, your local English Heritage Office and Conservation Offices or contact the National Lottery and your local Arts Board (Arts Council) to find out who they have funded in your area.

Experimenting with media

 By experimenting with art materials you learn how to improve your work.

 The more media you learn how to use, the more interesting your work will be.

Take risks with media

Many artists like to experiment with the media they use.

- They try and 'break the rules' by using material in a way that was never intended or by using something not normally associated with art – such as pebbles or snow.
- Artists have always liked to use new materials and technologies.
- When photography was invented in the nineteenth century, it was thought that no one would want to paint realistic pictures any more. Not only has realistic painting flourished, but artists who turned to photography have also created new forms of art and design.

A chance to be creative

As you become more successful and your confidence grows, you can 'push the boundaries' a bit and break the rules or make up new rules.

- This comes from experimenting with art media and using combinations in new and exciting ways.
- Experiments don't always work of course, and you might end up with a mess or two, but you are likely to have some successes along the way that give you more confidence.

>> **key fact** Remember that the material you work on and the combination of different media you use make a difference to the effect you get.

- The **ground** or **support** is as important as the medium.
- Ink dripped on absorbent **newsprint** is different to ink dripped on shiny card. Whether the card or paper is lying flat on a table or pinned to a vertical board makes a difference too!

What works for one artist doesn't necessarily work for another – try anything and everything and go with what works for you.
Paul Dixon

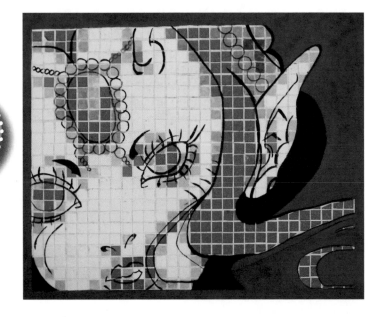

Digital graphics, mixed media on canvas

Learning from your experimentation

It's not enough to experiment for experiment's sake, even though this is a good place to start!

- You will need to **record** that you have learned from your experiments.
- A few notes or annotations, reminding you of what you did and whether you think it worked or not are important.

>> **key fact** **Don't be tempted to destroy something that you feel has gone 'wrong'. If it was a genuine experiment, trying something new with art materials, it can't actually go 'wrong'. You might end up with an effect you didn't expect and don't want to use, that's all.**

Avoid labels and headings

Labels and headings are not necessary.

- Examiners do not need to see a page titled 'My Experiments with Media': they can work that out for themselves. It might even count against you if it looks like you have done this for the examiner rather than as a genuine attempt to come up with new ways of using art materials for your work. After all the 'examiner' is your teacher – you don't need to tell your teacher things they know already!
- Similarly, you don't need to identify the materials you are experimenting with unless you think you are likely to forget!
- Only label unusual media or different types of the same medium that are so similar that you might not remember.
- **Examiners know what they are looking at and don't need to be told.**

Media to experiment with

Try **different combinations**, on top and over each other, and on different surfaces, and paste the results into your work journal.

Grounds/supports	Mark-making with dry media	Mark-making with wet media	Painting without brushes
<ul><li>Paper: cartridge, newsprint, copier, blotting, watercolour, wallpaper, sand, sugar, textured, handmade, tissue, tracing, parcel</li><li>Card: corrugated, white-faced, strawboard, pulp board</li><li>Board: MDF, hardboard, canvas</li></ul>	<ul><li>Pencils and graphite: hard, soft, sharp, fine, bold</li><li>Chalk and charcoal</li><li>Soft artist's pastels</li><li>Oil pastels (paint on a stick!)</li><li>Drawing with an eraser (shade an area with graphite and 'draw' by rubbing out)</li></ul>	<ul><li>Inks and dyes: coloured, Indian, fabric, Brusho pigments</li><li>Paint: poster, gouache, watercolour, acrylic, PVA</li><li>Household emulsion paint</li><li>Spirit based paint</li></ul>	<ul><li>Sponges</li><li>Toothbrush-flicking</li><li>Cotton buds</li><li>Palette knives</li><li>Credit cards</li><li>Squeegees</li><li>Painting rollers</li><li>Blowing through straws</li><li>Fingers</li></ul>

Improving your work

 Keep track of progress.

 Explain your work.

 Use what you've learnt to make your work better.

Making your work better as you do it

This is an important part of Assessment Objective 2, and many marks can be lost if it is not clear how you have made your work better as you did it.

- If you rub out all your 'mistakes' the examiner won't be able to see what you learnt by making them!
- Keep notes, such as in a diary, to record your work as it develops. These notes should be added to the bottom of the relevant pages of your work journal.
- Use them to look back on what you did in a lesson or at home.

In the preparation period before the exam it is a good idea to get into the habit of making **tracings** of, or **photocopying**, your work as it goes through different stages.

Carnival, **mixed media on canvas**

- You can add comments to the copies explaining what you did.
- Include these in your work journal to show the progress you made.

>> key fact Think of this aspect of GCSE Assessment as saving your work when you use a computer. If the machine crashes, you risk losing the lot if you haven't saved it. Don't let this happen to your artwork.

An example of work journal notes

Finished two observation drawings of my cat asleep on a rug – the first one in pencil I found difficult, the proportion was wrong because her head was too big. For the second study I moved to a different position and it was easier to get the shape right – this was good because I used a black fineliner and couldn't rub it out. I also found this good to draw fur in short strokes following the shape of the cat's body. I will use this technique on my drawing of the lion I am doing next lesson.

If you chase perfection, you often catch excellence.
William Fowble

Increasing your confidence

Making tracings and copies encourages you to experiment without the risk of 'spoiling' your work.

- Different media and **techniques** can be tested and practised on the copies.
- If your work is not easily copied, whether too big to fit on the copier or 3-D, use a **digital camera** or **camera phone**. You can experiment with the work in progress and record the stages the work goes through. The software may allow you to add your comments as notes.
- Print these pictures out and paste them in your work journal.

Making comments, both positive and negative

Show examiners what you have learnt during the course and how you put it into practice to make your work better.

- Don't fall into the trap of simply saying what you enjoyed doing and what you didn't. It might be nice to know that you enjoy art, but, unfortunately, you don't get marks for it!
- If you enjoyed trying something new that worked better than you expected, and are planning to use the technique for your final exam, so much the better!

>> **key fact** **How well you use the language of art, craft and design, whether spoken or written down, is very important because it shows how much you understand about the subject, not just about what you can do.**

Language has a scale of different levels, and the further you get up this scale, the higher your GCSE grade is likely to be.

study hint >>

If you are more confident speaking than writing, record your comments.

1	list	6	explain
2	describe	7	propose
3	sort	8	discuss
4	make comparisons	9	make judgements
5	make connections	10	justify

Use the key words in this list to make sure you are showing your full potential.
For example, if a friend asks you what you are doing for your GCSE Art exam, do you:

1. give them a list of the things you plan to do?
2. describe what you intend to do?
3. bring out examples of things you are doing?
4. show them different ideas, some better than others?
5. show how your ideas have been sparked off from your research?
6. explain, in detail, the stages you are planning to go through?
7. give them some hints so they can work it out for themselves?
8. share your ideas with them and ask for their ideas as well?
9. explain how your work fits the assessment objectives for GCSE?
10. show and explain your plans giving reasons why you've done it that way?
11. do all of the above?!

Mixed media and 3-D processes

- When experimenting with media, get into the spirit of it and don't be afraid to try new things.

- Plan out how you want your work to be presented.

- There are three main ways of working in 3-D: carving, modelling and construction.

Mixed media

Using mixed media seems a modern way of making art, but it has a long history going back as far as Leonardo da Vinci (1452–1519), who used experimental techniques in the fifteenth and sixteenth centuries.

- If you like to experiment with media you could research the following artists: Gustav Klimt (1862–1918), Pablo Picasso (1881–1973), George Braque (1882–1963), Robert Rauschenberg (1925–2008), Edward Kienholz (1927–94) and Jane Frank (1918–86).

study hint >>

The idea of layering is a key one in mixed media approaches to art. Build up the image by overlaying different materials, colours, tones and shapes to create the desired effect.

>> **key fact** Mixed media is not just about using different materials for different parts of a picture – this approach is more like collage; have a look at Kurt Schwitters' (1887–1948) *Merz Pictures* series.

Carving

Starting with a block of suitable material (**polystyrene**, **plaster**, **wood**, **building blocks**, **dried-out clay**), you cut, carve, scrape and chip away the parts you don't want.

- The **form** you are left with is the finished work.
- Carving is perhaps the most difficult 3-D process to master and it is the one that examiners see least of.
- It takes practice and experience to know which parts to carve away. Mistakes can't be easily put right!

remember >>

It is important to keep tools sharp when carving. Blunt tools lack precision and are harder to use, making mistakes and accidents more common.

Transport Mural, panel design, mixed media

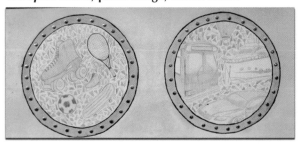

Still life, mixed media experiment

study hint >>

Start with small pieces and soft materials and, as your experience and confidence grow, work with larger and with more difficult materials.

Modelling

This is the most common form of 3-D work, where you use a **plastic** material to mould and shape with your hands.

- The best plastic material is clay, of which there are different types.
- Use clay that has **grog** in it, tiny bits of fired clay that make the clay feel 'gritty' and that give it more 'body'.

The finish on your model is as important as the shape and form of it. You must decide the surface effect you want to achieve: a smooth or rough finish, brightly coloured and varnished, or one where the material is left in its fired state, undecorated.

study hint >>

Air-dry clays do not need expensive **kilns** to **fire** them or **glazes** to finish them off.

>> **key fact** Ceramics sculptors and craftworkers are always trying new combinations of material and processes. It is very much part of the 'culture' of the craft to be experimental.

Construction

The range of materials you can use to construct 3-D objects is vast, making it perfect for **recycling**. This is not making art from 'rubbish'. You actually need a wide range of different materials to choose from. Here are some examples:

- wood off-cuts
- plastics
- wire and cable
- glass
- metal
- tubing
- card
- sheet materials.

Think of how your 3-D work will be supported while you make it. The easiest way is to use a **vice-grip** or **workmate**, but you might hang it from a hook in the ceiling or even make a temporary **'cradle'** to hold it that can be dismantled and discarded when the work is finished.

Traditionally, 3-D work is presented on a **stand**, **block** or **podium**. This is the equivalent of framing or mounting a picture when it's finished. You must consider this as you work.

study hint >>

You need a good range of tools to cut and shape materials as well as the means to join them together permanently. Try
- **hot glue guns**
- **resin**
- **pop riveters**
- **soldering irons**
- **nails and screws.**

Hands, wire and plaster constructions

Improving your visual research skills

- Drawing is the key.
- Mark-making is experimenting with drawing media.
- Work from first-hand observation.

What drawing is, and what drawing isn't

At its most simple, **drawing** is no more than marking a surface with a material. Doodling is drawing, where you allow your mind to meander and play around with lines and shape and forms. Paul Klee (1879-1940) used this technique as a starting point for his work. He called it 'taking a line for a walk', letting it show him where it wanted to go.

Everyone can draw, in their own way. The people who can draw the best are those who can draw in a range of ways. Are you good at drawing maps or plans? This is a different type of drawing to realistic pictures drawn and shaded with pencils.

- Drawing helps you **visualise** your ideas and explain them to others. It gets the ideas out of your head onto the paper.

>> **key fact** If you are prepared to learn the 'rules' and practise drawing, you will get better and better at it.

remember >>

Drawing is a skill you need to practise, not something you are born with!

Experimenting with different techniques

It might help to think of drawing as **mark-making** – this is how many artists see it. How many different kinds of mark can you make with a simple drawing tool? Take a pencil, for example.

- The lead (**graphite**) could be sharp or blunt, it could be a soft **grade** (2B, 3B, 4B) with dark lines and shading or it could be a hard grade – good for crisp lines and **cross-hatching** but not for tones.
- You could use the side of the lead instead of the point. You could make dots and dashes, thick, thin, long and short lines, straight, zigzag, wavy or flowing ones.
- You could mix some of these together.
- Now try coloured crayons, watercolour pencils, a fineliner, a felt marker…

study hint >>

Fill up pages in your work journal with experiments like these, and then use them for reference as you work. When you are just about to start a drawing, have a look at your 'experiment page' and pick a technique or a medium.

Smiley, ideas development, work journal pages

Observation

Most people take seeing pretty much for granted; after all, you use your eyes all the time, don't you?

- But when was the last time you really observed something?
- The point about observation is that it should make you 'focus in' on the subject you are drawing so that you begin to understand how it is made, and not just what its outside surface is like.

Time yourself while you are drawing.

- You should spend almost the same amount of time looking as actually drawing.
- Most students will glance up at the objects they are drawing and spend most of the time with their eyes on the paper.
- Don't fall into this habit! You are actually drawing from memory which is much more difficult, and not really necessary, when the subject is actually right in front of you!

study hint >>

Professional portrait artists learn about the shape of the skull and how muscles and skin tissues are formed over it, as well as how to paint the person as they look on the outside.

Different types of drawing

- Recording and communicating information: what something looks like
- Analytical: how something is made
- Exploring: trying out and experimenting with different drawing tools
- Expressing emotions: getting your feelings out onto the page
- Showing space, overlaps and differences in emphasis
- Showing the third dimension: perspective and changes in scale
- Decorating: adding patterns and adornment

study hint >>

- **Practise mark-making before you start drawing.**
- **Use a range of different drawing materials.**
- **Choose subjects that interest you.**
- **Think about what you want your drawing to say.**
- **Avoid too much rubbing out: mistakes show you are learning!**
- **Annotate your drawing with a few key words.**

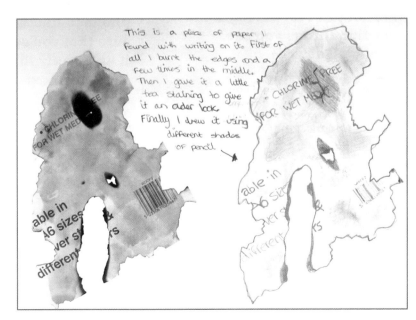

Work journal page: drawing study of paper burnt and stained to give an ageing effect

Making good use of ICT

- You can use **information and communication technology** (ICT) at any stage.

- Good use of the **World Wide Web** can help make you more creative.

Using computers to improve your GCSE grade

You are probably familiar with using **CD-ROMs** or the World Wide Web to find out about the world of art and design, but ICT can be used in many more ways than this.

- ICT can help you develop your ideas and record that process – in effect, a digital work journal!
- ICT can be used to change and play with images and to transfer them from one medium to another.
- ICT is particularly good for experimenting with different effects of colour and tone.
- Consider ICT as a new medium giving different outcomes in its own right.

>> **key fact** Conventional artwork can be photographed and you can make a multimedia presentation, an online gallery or posters to advertise an exhibition.

study hint >>

You can use ICT to research, create, alter and swap images about.

Digital cameras

Digital cameras can be used for primary research into your GCSE theme.

>> **key fact** Taking your own photographs counts as primary research, but you shouldn't let photographs be your only means of recording things you see. Drawing and painting is expected as well.

- Try using digital photography to record your work as you do it, especially if it goes though several different stages, such as a printing process, or modelling a sculptural form from clay.
- It's also useful for keeping a record of your work if the stages it goes through change it forever, as when carving out a form from a solid block or firing claywork in the kiln.

Other uses of digital photography are:

- recording different views around any piece of 3-D work
- recording your contribution to a group project to include in your work journal.

study hint >>

If you have to move a still life display, take photographs of it using your mobile phone to make sure that you set it up exactly the same the next time.

Cameras record, artists interpret.
Andrew Hamilton

CD-ROMs

Many galleries have developed CD-ROMs or interactive websites that include activities and games to introduce you to particular artists, craft-workers and designers and their styles, motivations and work methods. These can be entertaining as well as informative and can give you ideas to develop yourself.

study hint >>

Many CD-ROMs allow you to make a personal scrapbook or album of pictures from their collection. Use this facility to make up a selection of images linked to your GCSE theme or topic.

Research using the World Wide Web

The Internet can be an effective use of time or an effective waste of time, depending on how good you are at using it! Have a clear idea what you are looking for.

- More and more Internet sites have ways of working that are good for GCSE research. For example **www.wga.hu** has a **dual viewer** facility where you can compare two pictures on the same theme or view an artist's biography at the same time as examples of their work.

>> **key fact** If your final outcome is presented as a web page you could include links to other websites or pages that you used for your initial research.

(See page 5 for a list of useful websites)

study hint >>

For a free online tutorial about how to use the Internet to research art and design, visit **www.vts.rdn. ac.uk/tutorial/ media.**

Being creative and experimenting with art media

Computer **software** for painting and drawing is very advanced, and you can achieve an effect on the screen that is very close to the effect the real material makes on paper.

- Programs such as 'Painter' by Corel Software mimic the different effects that different papers have on the media used.
- ICT tools can be useful for trying out art techniques and equipment that are not available to you in real life, such as **spray painting** or **airbrushing**, photography or **animation**.

The Internet also provides **interactive** websites with experimental activities for a range of art, craft and design processes. Examples are:

- Watch artists at work and have a go yourself at **www.artisancam.org.uk/home.php**
- Escher pattern-making: **http://escher.epfl.ch/escher**

study hint >>

Try downloading **Rainbox** from **www.axlrosen.net/rainbox. html** (if you have a Mac) or **Liquidpaint** from **http://rydia. net/udder/prog/lp** (if you have a PC). These free psychedelic painting programs are ideal for experimenting with ideas and images.

Connecting with other artists' work

- Making connections is not the same as copying.
- Learn what artists do and use this to inspire your own work.

Discovering the context and intention

study hint >>
Refresh your knowledge of history and world events by typing the date and place into an Internet search engine.

All art, craft or design is created for a purpose, a reason behind the work that drives the artist to create it. Here are some questions to ask about any work of art, craft or design:

- What is the purpose of the work?
- What was the reason that drove the artist, craftworker or designer to create it?
- What was the context, or the setting, for the work?

Whether you are looking at a work of art, craft or design, the questions will give you some idea of the purpose behind it.

- Some reasons are not at all easy to read in a work of art and need time and thought to discover.
- Where and when the piece was made may give reasons for its existence.

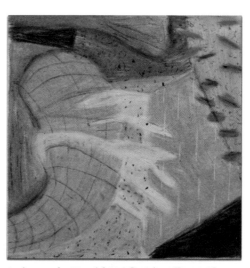

Artist study (David Hockney), oil pastel

Artist research (Andy Warhol),
work journal page

Artist study (Kandinsky), oil pastel

Subject matter that artists use for their work

One way of linking your work to another artist's is by using similar subject matter.

For example, under the theme of 'Identity', you may decide to work on the idea of 'self-portrait'. Hundreds, if not thousands, of artists from Rembrandt in 1630 right up to Cindy Sherman today have produced compelling images of themselves for many different reasons and in many different styles.

Art educationalist Rod Taylor suggests the following categories for themes that occur throughout the world of art, craft and design.

1 Human experience	**4 Events**
1.1 Self (identity)	4.1 Historical events
1.2 Family	4.2 Personal experiences
1.3 Relationships	4.3 Community life
2 The environment	**5 Fantastic and strange**
2.1 Natural (landscape, seascape)	5.1 Myths, legends and fairy tales
2.2 Man-made (external/internal)	5.2 Metamorphosis and change
	5.3 Dreams
3 Animals and plants	**6 Abstraction**
3.1 Plant life (living/dead)	6.1 Shape, form and space
3.2 Animals, birds, fish, insects (living/dead)	6.2 Abstract expression and meaning
	6.3 Pattern and decoration.

Bicycle study merged with Kandinsky

study hint >>

Try making links with the following themes: 'Inside', 'Framed', 'Viewpoints', 'Lettering and Text', 'Contrasts', 'Fantastic and Strange'.

study hint >>

If the theme you are working on fits under one of these headings, you can find other art, craft and design work to help you develop and expand your own ideas.

Take up the SEMI approach

Use the **SEMI** approach to describe artworks. This will help you to describe, analyse and evaluate works of art, craft and design and increase your marks in AO1.

SEMI: Subject, Elements, Media, Intent

SEMI stands for **Subject**, **Elements**, **Media** and **Intent**.

- It is a simple acronym designed to help you remember four key things when looking at and trying to appreciate works of art, craft and design.
- Every single piece of art, craft or design work you can find, from anywhere, made at any time can be described using three (if not all four) of these headings.

Subject

The subject matter of a work of art is not just what the work IS, but what it is ABOUT.

In 'realistic' painting, traditional subjects are portraits and figures, landscapes and still life. In crafts and design, the 'subject' might be more obvious – the subject matter of a fashion designer is clothes (or hats, shoes or accessories), and the subject matter of an architect is buildings or public spaces such as airports, shopping centres or churches. Other designers might focus on interior design or gardens.

- What is the work about?
- What is its subject matter?
- Was it **observed** first-hand, **remembered** or **imagined**?
- Is it realistic, or distorted to make it more abstract? Can you say why?
- Could there be any hidden, or at least disguised, **meanings** lying under the surface?
- Can you 'read' the artwork to discover if it is about more than it seems at first glance?

> *If I could say it in words, there would be no reason to paint.*
> **Edward Hopper**

> *Everybody has his own interpretation of a painting he sees.*
> **Francis Bacon**

Elements

If you break down works of art you have the **visual and tactile elements**.
The elements are line, colour, tone, pattern, texture, shape, form and space.

- How is it arranged?
- What kind of **colour scheme** did the artist use? Do the colours match or clash?
- Does it have one main shape or form?
- Is it made up from different shapes joined together?
- Is the work the same all over or does it have particular **features** that stand out and draw your attention to them?

study hint >>

Use the 'critical vocabulary' on pages 64–5 to find terms to describe art objects. These terms have a special meaning for GCSE students and professional artists alike.

Media

In art terms, **'media'** means the materials used by artists to create their work. Sometimes the media and the process used is obvious, but sometimes you need to have been through the process yourself to appreciate what the artist has done. Otherwise you have to guess!

- How was the work made and what was it made with?
- What **materials**, **tools** and **techniques** did the artist use?
- How did the artist start? Where do you think the artist finished?
- Has the artist used designs, sketches, photographs or other studies to help with the work?
- What **skills** must the artist have to create the work?
- Do you think it took a long time, or was it done quickly?

I found I could say things with colour and shapes that I couldn't say any other way – things I had no words for.
Georgia O'Keeffe

Intent

What drove the artist to create the work in the first place? What was the artist's intention? Unless you can do some research into the artist and their work, you might find this question difficult.

- What is the **purpose** of the work?
- Does it achieve its purpose?
- Is it a work of its time?
- Does the **context** of the work give you any clues to the artist's intention?
- What do you think the artist was **feeling** when working on it?
- Does the work **affect** you in any way? Do you like or dislike it? Can you say why?

Worksheet

Here is an example of a worksheet designed to help you describe, analyse and evaluate paintings – an example with more details and explanation is given on the next page.

Name .... Tutor Group .... Art Group ....

Artwork Title .... Artist .... Date ....

In this picture I can see ....

....

In the background there is ....

....

In the middle distance I can see …...

....

In the foreground there are ....

....

Overall I can describe the artwork as ....

....

The lines and shapes are ....

....

The colours are ....

....

I can also see textures and patterns that are ....

....

I think the way the artist made this artwork was by ....

....

The first part the artist did was ....

....

Then the artist ....

....

Finally the artist ....

....

The picture makes me feel ....

....

Before I started looking closely at this picture I thought ....

....

Now I have looked more closely I think ....

....

Name .... Tutor Group .... Art Group ....

Artwork Title .... Artist .... Date ....

In this picture I can see
Describe exactly what you can see. Don't worry if it seems obvious – in fact the more obvious the better. You need to do this before going on to more difficult and analytical statements.

In the background there is
The atmosphere of a picture is often set by the background – whether a landscape or an abstract composition.

In the middle distance I can see
This is not the setting (background) or the main subject (foreground), but everything else.

In the foreground there are
There are usually shapes, objects or people in the foreground; the artist wants to draw attention to them.

Overall I can describe the artwork as
Describe the structure, form and composition of the artwork.

The lines and shapes are
Are they rhythmic or chaotic?

The colours are
Soft and subtle? Pastel and tonal? Bright and 'in your face'? Strident and clashing? Or somewhere in between? Colour is very personal and changes with mood and fashion.

I can also see textures and patterns that are
Patterns can be seen but textures need to be felt or imagined.

I think the way the artist made this artwork was by
Try to find this out by looking up the information. Often the artwork has its material described next to the title: 'oil on canvas' or 'mixed media on board'.

The first part the artist did was
Guess! How does your work start? Sketches? Photographs? Drawing it out and then painting in?

Then the artist
Imagine the process the work went through – these could be in stages or overlapping layers.

Finally the artist
Did the artist finish the work? Did they take the idea a little bit further? Just when is a work of art finished?

The picture makes me feel
Any personal response is relevant, from sick to ecstatic! What do you think the artist wanted you to feel?

Before I started looking closely at this picture I thought
You must have been drawn to the work in the first place by something about it: what was that?

Now I have looked more closely I think
This statement is an important one. If you now know something about the work you didn't before, even if you don't like it any more than you did at first, you have learnt something which you could apply to your own artwork.

Using other artists' ideas

 You can find ideas, inspiration, topics and techniques to use for yourself by looking at the work of other artists.

Inspiration from the past

Looking back to the art, craft and design of the past is something that all artists do. You can find plenty of similarities to your own work and ideas as well as new ways of working that inspire you to have a go at something different.

There are some themes that artists have used in their work over and over again, here are some that you might like to try for yourself:

- the power of the portrait
- everyday life and times
- political cartoons and caricatures
- artists and designers in society today
- decorative, useful or applied arts
- modern designers and traditional craftworkers
- the difference between the arts and science
- representing reality or expressing abstract ideas
- art for everyone or art for the rich and famous.

Transcriptions versus copies

One way to learn about art and design is to study the work that interests and inspires you.

- The simplest way to understand another artist's work is to copy it, but simply copying somebody else's work – whether they are a famous artist or not – only goes so far in helping you to appreciate the artist.
- Take the idea further and create a **transcription** of the work you are studying.

>> **key fact** 'To transcribe' means to make a version of a picture, sculpture, craftwork or design object in a different material to the original. In this way you are always making something new and personal, even though the starting point was another artist's work.

- **Crop** a section or sections from the original and make transcriptions of the parts you have chosen. Focus in on a **detail** that is interesting in its own right.
- Find a section within an artwork that is relevant to the theme you are working on.
- Crop several different areas and transcribe them into your work journal using different media for each one.

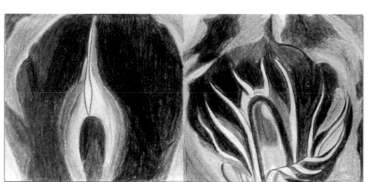

It's a poor artist who borrows – a good artist steals.
Pablo Picasso

Study of flowers (after Georgia O'Keeffe)

Getting into the mind of …

As you begin to learn more about particular artists, craftworkers and designers you will appreciate their motivation, ways of working and intentions. In short you will begin to get into their mind and be much more confident making work that connects your work and theirs.

- Imagine Pablo Picasso was one of your classmates. How would he draw your best friend?
- How might Georgia O'Keeffe use the theme 'Natural World' if she was doing GCSE?
- If Jackson Pollock was in your GCSE group, how would he decorate the front of his work journal?
- What would the school uniform be like if Vivienne Westwood designed it?

Making connections work for you

Looking closely at the work of other artists, craftworkers and designers, and learning more about them, can help you to take your own work further.

- All artists use other artists' work to learn from and get ideas.
- This is not considered 'cheating' unless all the artist does is copy the other work and pass it off as their own, which is **forgery**.
- You can take the earlier artist's ideas further and make them your own, or you can do just the opposite – a reaction to the work.

Not so long ago, any student wanting to become a fully trained artist would have to study and virtually copy famous works of art. It was thought that if you could mimic the techniques of the most highly regarded artists of the past, you could become an artist in your own right.

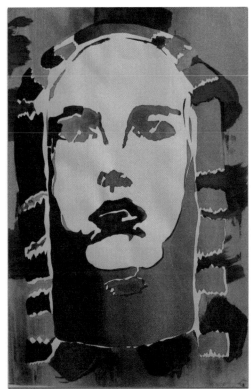

The Bridesmaid (after Sir John Everett Millais), Pre-Raphaelite, screen-print

Barriers to the truth (after Barbara Kruger), mixed media on panel

How to use the art history pages

Making links

The next 32 pages are designed to help you find some connections between your work and that of other artists, craftsworkers and designers. There are 8 sections, each with over 48 possible links to your own work to follow up. 8 x 48 equates to **384** ways of connecting your work to others covering all aspects of art, craft and design from prehistory to the present day!

The charts include:

A for ART (painting, sculpture, installations, environmental art, film & photography);

C for CRAFT (pottery, woodwork, printmaking, jewellery, masks and textiles);

D for DESIGN (fashion, graphics, computer art, theatre design and architecture).

The charts include a timeline to help you see the connections in relation to their period in history.

Each chart is laid out in the same way so you can easily find similarities and differences between the artwork listed and your own.

Headings that use the SEMI approach to study (see pages 16–17)

Key: tells you if the work is art, craft or design

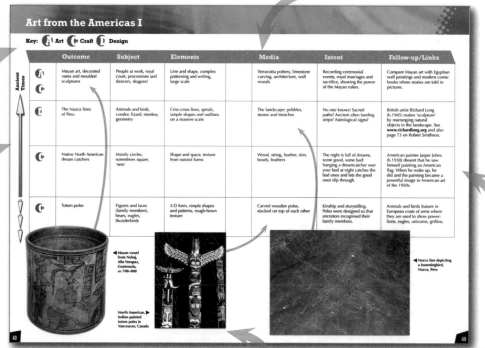

Timeline: gives you an idea of how old the work is

Images: examples chosen to illustrate descriptions

Follow-up/Links: examples of 'thinking sideways' and creative links

Making a list of words

Before you use the charts on the following pages you need to do some background work.

In your work journal write down a list of words that describe:

Subject matter – your theme or set task;
Elements – your favourite aspects of visual language: colour, pattern or form, for example;
Media – how you work best in 2-D or 3-D;
Intent – what you are aiming towards; what your final outcome *might* be.

Then using this list go on to cross-referencing …

Cross-referencing

Using the list of words you have written down, scan through the charts on pages 26–59 and try to find the **same words**. When you find them on a chart you then track along the row to the first and last columns where you will find a topic to research that will link in some way to your own work.

The possibilities are endless – well, at least 384 anyway!

Where to find out more

As we have learnt already, you get more marks if your research goes further than simply using what is to hand. You must follow up the links thoroughly to make proper use of them in your work. Use the facilities available to you at your school or in your neighbourhood, and ask people to help you with the topic you are researching. One GCSE student researching African art was surprised to discover that his geography teacher had a collection of masks and wooden sculptures from the year she spent working in a Kenyan school during her gap year. Other places to start your research include:

- the art department book collection;
- the school resource centre and library;
- the Internet (there is a list of websites on page 5, but GCSE Art and Design papers also have lists of websites to follow up);
- your local public library or local college/university libraries;
- art galleries and museums;
- artists studios – some have 'open studio' events where you can visit artists at work;
- stately homes, churches or cathedrals – crammed full of works of art and craft;
- your local town hall, tourist information centre, civic or arts centre – these often have short-term exhibitions and links to other sources of information.

Art is a powerful vehicle of communication. It can tell a story, convey a mood, or be a visual autobiography of the artist.
Rachel Rubin Wolf

Art from Africa I

Key:

Ancient Times

	Outcome	Subject	Elements
(D)	Meriotic pottery Sudan 100 BC	Pots with geometric designs, plants, animals and stick figures	Spherical shapes, simple line patterns
(A)	Egyptian art at the time of the Pharaohs	Figures and animals, scenes from everyday life and worship	Overlapping shapes suggesting space, proportion
(C)	Adornment and jewellery (necklaces and bracelets)	Animals, birds and insects, hieroglyphic writing signs and symbols	Symmetrical and symbolic patterns and shapes
(C)	Ceremonial masks	Human and animal faces, good and evil spirits, birds	Symmetrical shapes, geometrical lines and patterns, earth colours

Tso elephant mask from the Cameroon grasslands

28

Media	Intent	Follow-up/Links
Pottery painted with natural pigments	Pots meant life and death: new pots were made when a baby was born, old pots smashed when someone died.	Women made pots while men went hunting.
Pigments made from earth mixed with gum	Size indicates importance, not reality: kings and queens are really big!	'Ostracons' are small pieces of rock used by stonemasons to sketch out their designs before carving, a sort of Egyptian artist's work journal!
Gold, silver, semi-precious stones, cloisonné technique	Jewellery shows status and levels of importance, believed to make people god-like and immortal.	The scarab (dung beetle) was as sacred to the Egyptians as the Cross is to Christians.
Wood, fabric, skin, straw, feathers, beads, shells	Worshipping the spirits of the forest, blessings, rituals and funerals, protection from evil	Venetian carnival masks, Japanese theatrical masks, ancient Greek masks, Javanese dance masks

Egyptian ostracon, painted limestone found in Deir el-Medina dating from the 19th Dynasty

Art from Africa II

Key: Art Craft Design

	Outcome	Subject	Elements	
C **D**	Kuba textiles	Designs handed down in the family, ancestors can identify family members	Lines, diamonds, rectangles, symmetrical patterns, sombre earth colours	
C	Carved wooden figures	Male and female, woman and child, man with animal, outsider or stranger	Shape and 3-D form, smooth texture, burnished with glass, scratched patterns on the surface	
C **D**	Udu pottery drums	Clay round-hole pots used for making low 'heartbeat' drumming sounds	Spherical shapes, formed to make high or low notes, circular holes	
A	Ndidi Dike, Nigerian painter and sculptor	Traditional African motifs, the lizard and the tortoise, patterns from textiles	Very detailed sculptures with multi-layered textured surfaces and limited colours	

Today

Modern Yoruba door carving, Nigeria

Raffia dance skirt, Central Congo

Media	Intent	Follow-up/Links
Raffia, weaving, natural fibres and dyes, patchwork, appliqué, embroidery	Celebrations, funerals, currency, prestige	Henri Matisse (1869–1954) had a huge collection of Kuba cloth in his studio that inspired his painting.
Boxwood, ebony, oak, carvings are often 'smoked' to make them black	Tribal rituals for fertility, death, status, rites of passage, celebrations	Many English churches and cathedrals have fine wooden carvings on choir stalls and pews, including Ely, Wells and Lincoln cathedrals.
Hand-formed pottery with burnished surfaces, fired without being glazed	Designer Frank Giorgini creates modern drums based on traditional Nigerian technique.	You can hear Udu drums at **www.lpmusic.com/pros_that_play_lp/cd_reviews/garcia.html**.
Panelling and carved relief in stained wood, sculptures made from found objects	Bringing traditional ideas up to date. Showing the 'circle of life'.	Comparisons have been made with the constructions of Louise Nevelson (1899–1988).

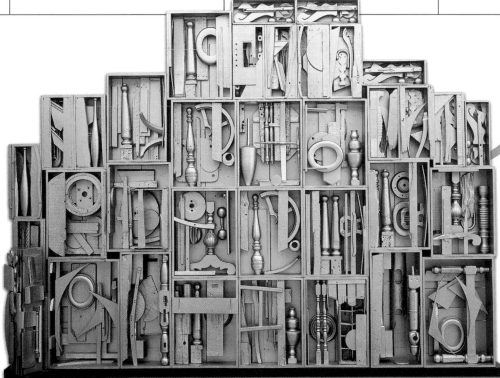

Royal Tide IV,
1959/60, found object construction, Louise Nevelson (1899–1988)

Art from the Americas I

	Outcome	Subject	Elements
A / **C**	Mayan art, decorated vases and moulded sculptures	People at work, royal court, processions and dancers, dragons!	Line and shape, complex patterning and writing, large scale
D	The Nazca lines of Peru	Animals and birds, condor, lizard, monkey, geometry	Criss-cross lines, spirals, simple shapes and outlines on a massive scale
C	Native North American dream catchers	Mainly circles, sometimes square, 'nets'	Shape and space, texture from natural forms
C	Totem poles	Figures and faces (family members), bears, eagles, thunderbirds	3-D form, simple shapes and patterns, rough-hewn texture

Ancient Times

Mayan vessel from Nebaj, Alta Verapaz, Guatemala, AD **700–800**

North American, Indian painted totem poles in Vancouver, Canada

Media	Intent	Follow-up/Links
Terracotta pottery, limestone carving, architecture, wall murals	Recording ceremonial events, royal marriages and sacrifice, showing the power of the Mayan rulers.	Compare Mayan art with Egyptian wall paintings and modern comic books where stories are told in pictures.
The landscape: pebbles, stones and trenches	No one knows! Sacred paths? Ancient alien landing strips? Astrological signs?	British artist Richard Long (b.1945) makes 'sculpture' by rearranging natural objects in the landscape. See **www.richardlong.org** and also page 57 on Robert Smithson.
Wood, string, leather, skin, beads, feathers	The night is full of dreams, some good, some bad: hanging a dreamcatcher over your bed at night catches the bad ones and lets the good ones slip through.	American painter Jasper Johns (b.1930) dreamt that he saw himself painting an American flag. When he woke up, he did and the painting became a powerful image in American art of the 1950s.
Carved wooden poles, stacked on top of each other	Kinship and storytelling. Poles were designed so that ancestors recognised their family members.	Animals and birds feature in European coats of arms where they are used to show power: lions, eagles, unicorns, griffins.

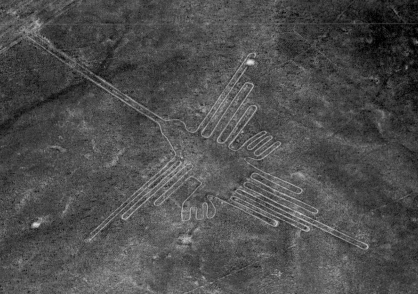

Nazca line depicting a hummingbird, Nazca, Peru

Art from the Americas II

	Outcome	Subject	Elements
A **D**	Mexican mural-painting, Diego Rivera (1886–1957)	Stories about the community and everyday life	Composition and arrangement of shapes, colours, tones and, most of all, scale!
A	Photography of Ansel Adams (1902–84)	American landscape in wide angle and close up	Tone, contrast, light and shade, minute detail and surface textures
D	DKNY, Donna Karan (b.1948), New York fashion designer	Clothes, fashion accessories with fruits and floral patterns	Style, colour, shape and form, soft textures and patterns
A	Chuck Close (b.1940)	Portraits of himself, his family and friends in 'super-realistic' style	Light and shade, tone and contrast, incredible 'photographic' detail, large scale

Today

Alex, **1991, ukiyo-e woodblock print, Chuck Close (b.1940)**

© Chuck Close, courtesy PaceWildenstein, New York

Media	Intent	Follow-up/Links
Fresco: paints mixed with plaster are used so that the finished picture is actually part of the wall, not painted on it.	Art that promotes revolution and political ideas, for example, the struggle for power between workers and the rich and powerful.	Diego Rivera was influenced by Pablo Picasso (1881–1973) and cubism, but also by the art of the Inca civilisation. See **www.riveramural.com** and **http://incas.perucultural.org.pe/ english/galeart106.htm**.
High-quality black and white (monochrome) photography	Shows the beauty of the wilderness and the importance of preserving it for the future.	An American painter working at the same time, Edward Hopper (1882–1967), painted landscapes and cityscapes that expressed loneliness and isolation.
Fashion design, illustration, advertising and marketing, packaging	Trend-setting, creating an image of relaxation. Fun, casual, soft and feminine	Check out **www.dkny.com** and **www.donnakaran.com** and the issues raised in advertising by FCUK at **www.fcuk.com/ fcukadvertising**.
As well as painting, Close uses different printmaking processes: woodblock and screen prints.	Very realistic pictures that look as if they are created by photography or computer, but are actually painted by hand.	Try Close's process and draw a picture of yourself by following the instructions at **www. princetonol.com/groups/iad/ lessons/middle/larry-valuegrid. htm**.

Detroit Industry (north wall detail), 1933, fresco, Diego Rivera (1886–1957)

© 2009 Banco de México Diego Rivera & Frida Kahlo Museums Trust, México, D.F., DACS.

Donna Karan fashion show, autumn 2005

Art from Asia and the East I

Ancient Times

	Outcome	Subject	Elements
C	Porcelain – known as 'china' because this is where it was invented	The landscape of China and Japan: gardens, trees, flowers, scenes from everyday life, fishes, birds and dragons	Flat perspective, predominant colour blue, pattern and shape
C **D**	Japanese samurai armour	Mainly for protection but also to scare and threaten enemies; often the shapes were based on human and animal anatomy.	Overlapping layers and jointed structures, fierce colours and patterning
C **D**	Hoysala sculpture and architecture from India	Hindu gods, dancing maidens, natural objects (leaves, winding branches, stems and flowers), scenes from everyday life	3-D forms made to fit agreed rules of proportion, balance, movement and structure.
A **C** **D**	Islamic tiles	Islamic teaching forbids pictures of people or animals, patterns are made from writing and plants or flowers.	Complex, ornate design of intertwined flowers, leaves and geometric figures called 'arabesque'.

Enamelled vase, Japanese school, nineteenth century

© Leeds Museums and Art Galleries (Temple Newsam House) UK

Samurai armour, Japan

Media	Intent	Follow-up/Links
Glazed, hand-painted pottery, pen and ink, enamelling, scrafitto	Buddhism and religious stories, myths and legends. Objects have symbolic meanings.	Grayson Perry (b.1960), the Turner Prize-winning ceramicist (2003) used traditional Chinese forms, but brought them right up to date with a controversial twist.
Bamboo frames, leather and cloth, beaten metal shapes	Designed to represent a code of warrior behaviour: loyalty, self-discipline and respect. The samurai sword was used to commit suicide rather than be captured.	Compare the shapes and forms with medieval suits of armour, a present-day soldier's battle kit and Darth Vader from Star Wars!
Stone carving with intricate piercing, fretwork on a massive scale	Carvings often represent strength, power, nobility and stability, religious meanings include the sacred river Ganges.	The best example is the Chennakeshva Temple in Belur. Many artists have used dance as a subject. Check out French artist, Edgar Degas' (1834–1917) ballet dancers, painted in the 1870s.
Highly glazed tiles, often with raised lines and brilliant inlaid colours, massed together on walls, floors and ceilings of mosques.	Many Islamic patterns represent the infinite, repeating themselves for ever. Spreading religious teaching, creating a feeling of experiencing 'heaven on earth'.	Islamic patterns 'tessellate', they have shapes that neatly fit into each other. For examples of tessellations, try **www.tessellations.org**.

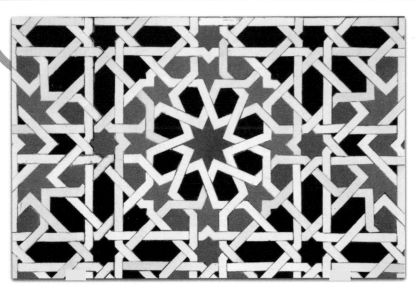

Ceramic tiles, Alcazar of Seville, Spain

Art from Asia and the East II

		Outcome	Subject	Elements
A **C**		Japanese woodblock printmaking	Landscapes and seascapes, houses, gardens and everyday scenes. Figures in traditional dress, animals, birds and plants	Flowing lines and clear-cut shapes, limited colours often blended and fading from one to another.
A **C**		Chinese brush painting and calligraphy	Chinese letterforms and symbols, plants – especially flowers, bamboo, trees (bonsai) – birds and fish	Flowing brushstroke lines with sweeping curves and carefully placed dots and dashes expressing rhythm and beauty, flat space perspective
A **D**		Bollywood film posters (Hindi)	Figures in action scenes, heroes and heroines, lettering and text	Changes in size and scale, complex compositions and perspective, strong light and shade, energetic and rhythmic arrangements.
A		Chinese experimental photography	Subjects are often the artist's own body, and record the experience of events.	Mainly light, shade and tone, but also action, movement and space.

Today

Blossoms (from Album of Fruit and Flowers), ink and colour on paper, **Chen Hongshou (1768–1821)**

Media	Intent	Follow-up/Links
Originally woodblock printing was a 'low' art form, something cheaply available for everyone – you didn't have to be rich to own a print! These were often printed in black and coloured by hand.	Pictures of ordinary and everyday life: people at work, families relaxing, playing, relationships. Outdoor scenes showing the weather and expressing moods.	The two most famous Japanese printmakers are Ando Hiroshige (1797–1858) and Katsushika Hokusai (1760–1849). Also look up **www.artelino.com/articles/japanese-woodblock-prints.asp**.
Chinese brushes with rabbit or sheep hair, water-based ink on paper or silk	Drawings show the artist's inner qualities of peace and harmony. Most pictures include a poem or inscription.	Chinese artists also invented paper-cut pictures, the forerunners of modern-day silkscreen printing. Look up **www.sino-arts.com** to see examples of Chinese art and craft.
Advertising graphics, painting and drawing, marketing	Capture all the different elements of the story of the film in one scene, show emotion and expression, drama and excitement or tenderness and love.	Posters are a neglected art form. They began around 1870 with the introduction of a 'lithographic' printing process and show great skill and imagination by the artist. See for yourself at **www.postershow.com**.
Digital and traditional chemical photography, film and video	Finding new forms of art and expressing views and opinions about society and the wider world.	An introduction to all forms of photography can be found at **www.masters-of-photography.com**.

Bollywood film poster

Awa Province Naruto rapids (from *Views of Famous Places in the Sixty Old Provinces*), **1855, print, Ando Hiroshige (1797–1858)**

Oceanic art I

Key: (A) Art (C) Craft (D) Design

	Outcome	Subject	Elements	
(A)	Aboriginal art, rock art, designs in sand, body art	Landforms, mountains and rivers, the weather, fire and water, animals and serpents	Lines and patterns made from dots of colour, 'X-ray' views through animals	
(C)	Solomon Islands shell carvings, Barava	Birds, animals, geometric patterns	Symmetrical patterns with repeated curved, circular and semicircular shapes	
(C) **(D)**	Melanesian wood carvings and ritual masks	Faces of the gods and spirit creatures, often with strong animal, insect or bird forms	Bright colours, generally symmetrical in form with inscribed lines for decoration	
(D)	Wayang puppets from Indonesia and Bali	Male and female dancers and characters from stories, myths and legends	Exaggerated and flattened shape, brightly coloured and with very decorative patterns	

Ancient Times

Rock art depicting a pig-nosed turtle, Kakaku National Park, Australia

Shadow puppets, Indonesia

Media	Intent	Follow-up/Links
Sand, bark, earth pigments, charcoal, scoring and engraving	'The Dreaming' represents balance and harmony between the spiritual, natural and man-made world.	French artist, Georges Seurat (1859–1891) painted dots of primary colours, in a style called 'pointillism' to create shimmering pictures.
Pierced, carved and shaped shells or shell fossils	Used as money (currency) to trade items, including brides and pigs, and as grave ornaments.	Look for Georgian intricate ivory fretwork fans (c.1830) and the craft of 'marquetry' (making delicate inlaid patterns with different woods).
Woods, rattan, natural pigments and dyes, skins and woven cloth	Designed for ritual use, rites of passage from boy to manhood, and from girl to womanhood.	Constantin Brancusi, Romanian abstract sculptor (1876–1957), made work in the style of Melanesian wood carvings.
Thin wooden sheets carved and pierced with intricate fretwork patterns	Traditional stories about farming, fertility and death, battles between gods and giants, good versus evil.	Look for puppets in other times and cultures: Burmese Monkey King, Pinocchio, The Muppets, Thunderbirds and Flat Eric!

The Kiss, 1907, stone, Constantin Brancusi (1876–1957)

© ADAGP, Paris and DACS, London 2009

Oceanic art II

	Outcome	Subject	Elements	
A	Maori tattoo	Symbolic seabirds, snakes and sharks' teeth. Clasping hands for unity and stars for good luck	Generally tonal with linking lines and shapes, swirls, spirals, waves and flame shapes	
A **D**	Outdoor installation art, design and architecture. Duke Albada (b.1967)	Site-specific environmental artworks in figurative and abstract forms	Creating unique spaces using 3-D forms, shape and projected light.	
A	Aboriginal art in galleries	Same traditional subjects, particularly the landscape seen from a bird's-eye view.	Stripes, lines, shapes and patterns made from dots and dashes	
A	Contemporary sculptor, Virginia King (b.1946)	The environment, ideas expressed in words and micro-organisms	Shape, form and texture, location and scale, positive and negative space	

Today

Hand drawn Aboriginal abstract depicting flowing water, kangaroo tracks and waterholes

Media	Intent	Follow-up/Links
Skin pierced with sharp tools and rubbed with dyes made from natural materials.	Designs are created to reflect the importance of the wearer. Mythical stories of heroism and bravery.	Traditional Maori designs are still used for tattoos today, as are Celtic forms, Chinese symbols, ancient scripts and signs of the zodiac.
Modern building materials including metal, glass and plastic as well as soap bubbles and light.	To improve the visual quality of particular places.	Duke Albada was born in the Netherlands and was influenced by the de Stijl design group and Piet Mondrian (1872–1944). You can view an animated film of Mondrian's art at **www.youtube. com/watch?v=i5kZL6_920g&featur e=related**.
A mix of modern and traditional art materials, bringing the art form up to date.	Keeping alive the spirit of the original Aboriginal stories and legends, showing how the native peoples have been affected by colonisation.	Look up paintings by Billy Stockman Tjapaltjarri (b.1925), Clifford Possum Tjapaltjarri (1932–2002) and Emily Kame Kngwarreye (1910–96).
Stone, bronze, steel, the earth and wood	Site-specific artwork (designed for a particular place) to make you think about what humans are doing to the environment.	Andy Goldsworthy (b.1956) is perhaps the UK's most well-known environmental artist. Compare King's work to his at **www. goldsworthy.cc.gla.ac.uk**.

Carving at Rotorua, New Zealand showing warrior face paint

European art, craft and design I

Key: **A** Art **C** Craft **D** Design

	Outcome	Subject	Elements
A	Cave paintings at Lascaux, France	Animals, nature, 'matchstick men', hunting	Line, shape, earth colours and tones
A **D**	'Renaissance man', Leonardo da Vinci (1452–1519)	Artist/painter, scientist/anatomist, inventor of flying machines and tanks	As a painter, Leonardo excelled in the use of light, shading and colour, called 'chiaroscuro'.
C **D**	Art nouveau, decorative style of the 1890s	Nature and twisting plant forms, growth, the opposite of straight lines and regularity	Flowing thick and thin lines and swirling shapes. Architecture, interior design and all forms of craft
A	Berthe Morisot (1841–1895), painter and printmaker	Women, sometimes with children, usually out of doors or in a domestic setting	Light through the use of colour and tone (she never used black)

Ancient Times

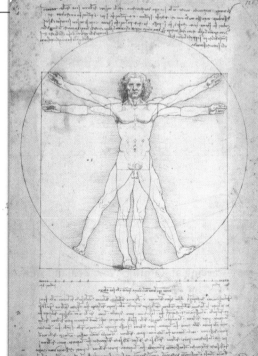

**Proportions of the human figure
(*Vitruvian Man*), c.1492, pen and ink on
paper, Leonardo da Vinci (1452–1519)**

Media	Intent	Follow-up/Links
Charcoal, pigments made from the earth, berries and fruits, finger painting, spraying by mouth.	Who knows? Showing how animals behave? Planning a hunt? Hoping for good luck? Storytelling? Appealing to the gods? Celebrations?	See for yourself at the official website **www.culture.gouv.fr/culture/arcnat/lascaux/en**. Swiss painter and sculptor Alberto Giacometti (1901–66) created thin stick-like figures of men and women that resemble the style of cave art.
Pen and ink, oil paint on wood, fresco technique on plaster	Whatever Leonardo did he tried to uncover the truth about the subject, what made it work, and why it was the way it was.	Leonardo was a vegetarian and an animal lover, and would often buy caged birds in the market just to set them free. Find out more at **www.mos.org/leonardo**.
Metal, glass, carved and shaped wood, pottery	Using materials in new ways to copy forms found in nature, bringing natural forms into the city.	Glassware by Rene Lalique (1860–1945); architecture by Antonio Gaudi (1852–1926) and artists such as Gustave Klimt (1862–1918) and Alphonso Mucha (1860–1939).
Worked in the open air using oil paints or chalk pastels	Create fresh, bright and happy impressions of contented home life.	Inspired by French impressionists, especially Édouard Manet (b.1832), her brother-in-law, known to finish her work off himself! What do you think of that?

The Cherry Picker, 1891, oil on canvas, Berthe Morisot (1841–1895)

Chimneys from the Antonio Gaudi designed building, La Pedrera, Barcelona, Spain

European art, craft and design II

Key: **A** Art **C** Craft **D** Design

	Outcome	Subject	Elements
A	Pointillism, painting pictures with dots of pure colour	Views across the land and sea, actors, actresses and circus performers	Colour and tone, light and shade, pattern and space
A	Abstraction, Piet Mondrian (1872–1944)	Mondrian started as a painter of landscapes and trees.	He emphasised the horizontal and vertical lines and filled in the spaces with plain colours.
A	Joseph Beuys (1921–86) German installation and conceptual artist	Pushing traditional artforms beyond normal boundaries. Art and life are not separate things; Beuys lived his art and art became his life.	Space, form, ideas, experience, the body (his body), ideas and emotions
A **D**	Pixel art, computer graphics, eBoy	Cities, vehicles, buildings, machines, airplanes	Isometric perspective, 3-D form and space

Today

PCHOME, eBoy, www.eboy.comcourtesy the artist

©1998–2005 eBoy (Steffen Sauerteig, Svend Smital, Peter Stemmler, Kai Vermehr)

Media	Intent	Follow-up/Links
Oil-painted dots, specks and dashes of bright colours that blend together when viewed from a distance.	Semi-scientific approach to art. You, the viewer, have to make the effort to 'finish' the picture off in your own mind as you look at it.	Georges Seurat (1859–91) invented the technique, Paul Signac (1863–1935) also used it. Photographs in magazines are printed using dots of ink: look at one using a magnifying glass.
Drawings in crayon, charcoal; paintings in watercolour, oil	Gradually reduced his compositions to the most basic simple geometric forms and primary colours.	For more information about him and to view a large collection of his work and developing style, look at **www.mondriantrust.com**.
Hard and soft materials including wood, metal and stone. All sorts of found junk, industrial felt, wax and animal fat.	Beuys lived his belief that art can change society; he was a philosopher as well as an artist.	Work included a Volkswagen van pulling some sledges. VW cars have featured a lot in art, for example see an example in Tom Wesselmann, *Landscape No.2*, on page 58.
All computer-drawn using 'Photoshop' software.	To represent popular culture: shopping, Lego, TV, toy commercials, computer games and the media.	Theo Van Doesburg (1883–1931) created isometric drawings in paint on paper for the de Stijl group in 1923.

Pine Tree at St Tropez,
1909, oil on canvas, Paul
Signac (1863–1935)

Art, craft and design in the UK I

Key: 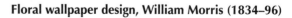 **A** Art **C** Craft **D** Design

		Outcome	Subject	Elements
Ancient Times	**A**	The megalith at Stonehenge	A ceremonial place for ritual and worship, a sort of prehistoric cathedral	Circular shape, 3-D form on a huge scale creating an open space, balance
	A **C**	Celtic art	Abstract patterns (originally from Italy and Greece), animals, including dogs and snakes	A mixture of complicated asymmetrical (unbalanced) and overlapping forms, and some symmetrical geometric interlocking shapes.
	A	Romantic landscape painting, J.M.W. Turner (1775–1851)	English castles, seascapes, sunrise and sunset, trains and ships	The effects of light and shade, colour and tone, and more colour.
	D	Wallpaper and textiles of the Arts and Crafts period	Natural forms such as plants, leaves, flowers, birds	Style and all-over patterning, rich and tonal colour combinations, natural shapes and forms

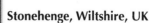

Floral wallpaper design, William Morris (1834–96)

Stonehenge, Wiltshire, UK

48

Media	Intent	Follow-up/Links
Stone, earth, alignment with the sun, construction	A place for rituals, ceremonies, the summer solstice and forms of pagan worship, druids use it nowadays but it was built long before druids or Celts ever came to Britain.	Make connections with Land Art of the 1960s and 1970s, Walter de Maria (b.1935) (see **www.lightningfield.org**), Robert Smithson (1938–73) and Robert Morris (b.1931).
Illuminated manuscripts, highly decorated written pieces, stone and woodcarving, jewellery. Ordinary and everyday objects were often decorated with bands of Celtic design, found today in tattoos.	Try following the moving pictures on the knot plot website, **www.knotplot.com**.	Try weaving some knots using unconventional materials: wire, plastic, straw, twigs.
Pen, pencil and watercolour sketches in his own work journal (*Liber studorium*), oil-painting and etching	Turner tried to capture the atmospheric effect of light on his subjects and is considered to be one of the greatest English artists.	Turner's friend and art critic, John Ruskin (1819–1900) called him the painter of light – this idea influenced the French impressionists.
Hand-printed wallpapers, woven hangings and textiles for interior decoration	Good design not just for the rich; well-designed and aesthetic (beautiful) environments available to all.	William Morris (1834–96) led this movement, but many others built on it, such as Charles Rennie Mackintosh (1868–1967) and the Pre-Raphaelite artists. The designs are still available today, from **www.achome. co.uk**.

The "Fighting Temeraire" Tugged to her Last Berth to be broken up, **before 1839, oil on canvas, Joseph Mallord William Turner (1775–1851)**

Art, craft and design in the UK II

Key: Art Craft ⊙ Design

	Outcome	Subject	Elements	
Ⓐ	Pop art and collage, Richard Hamilton (b.1922)	Items from modern everyday life, advertising	Composition and 'juxtaposition', putting things next to each other that you wouldn't normally see.	
Ⓓ	Extreme fashion design, Vivienne Westwood (b.1941)	Clothes, shoes, hats, accessories, jewellery, perfume for men and women	Clashing colours and striking patterns, strange shapes	
Ⓐ	Installation sculpture, Anish Kapoor (b.1954)	Abstract man-made forms and shapes inspired by natural objects	Large-scale 3-D forms, intense colouring, space and structure	
Ⓒ	Primavera contemporary crafts	Jewellery, ceramics, glass, textiles, metal work, furniture	Well-balanced shapes and forms, tactile surfaces, one-offs, subtle colour combinations	

Today

'Just what is it that makes today's homes so different, so appealing?', 1956, collage, Richard Hamilton (b.1922)

Media	Intent	Follow-up/Links
Collage: a picture made up by putting together other pictures, photographs and objects	Pop art took everyday things and raised them to the level of works of art by making an exhibition of them.	Richard Hamilton is interested in a group of artists called 'Dada' c.1916–22, Marcel Duchamp (1887–1968) in particular, to the extent of recreating a famous example of his work. Can you find out which one?
Printed fabrics, leather and suede, zips and safety pins, extreme make-up and hairstyles	Inspired by rock 'n' roll and punk music, designed to shock the public and put ideas of high street fashion through the mincer!	Vivienne Westwood: 'It's so important to look to the past, because people had taste and ideas of excellence'. Find out more at **www.viviennewestwood.co.uk**.
Sandstone, marble, slate, often drenched in pure powder pigments	Designed to promote calm contemplation and inner spiritual peace.	Try the following websites: **www.anishkapoor.com**; **www.tate.org.uk/tateetc/issue3/butisitinstallationart.htm**; **www.zhangyaxi.com/monumental_cast_concrete_sculpture_outdoor_public_sculpture_Qinghai_China.html**.
Often crafts workers use a mix of traditional craft processes, such as pottery and weaving, wood and metalwork, with modern materials.	Unique objects that are useful as well as artistically decorative, the type you prefer to look at rather than actually use.	Britain has a long tradition of producing acclaimed crafts workers such as textile designer Michael Brennand-Wood (b.1952) and jewellery-maker, Jane Adam (b.1954). Find out more at **www.artandcrafts.co.uk** and **www.kettlesyard.co.uk**.

Bone china textured veil bowl, **12 cm h by Sasha Wardell, courtesy the artist, photographer Mark Lawrence**

Key: **Art** **Craft** D **Design**

The 1700s

	Outcome	Subject	Elements
A	Botanical illustration, Maria Sibylla Merian (1647–1717)	Flowers and plants, butterflies and other insects	Accurate shape and form, colour and tone, incredible detail drawn and painted from direct observation.
D	Art deco furniture design, Eileen Gray (1879–1976)	Chairs, tables, screens, beds, sofas, rugs	Simple asymmetrical geometric shape and form, unconventional colour combinations. Famous for high-gloss shiny surfaces on wood, chrome, leather, industrial materials.
A	Op art, Bridget Riley (b.1931)	Abstract paintings often with strong visual effects. Originally worked in black and white, turning to colour in 1966.	Lines, wavy and straight, positive and negative space, movement, hard edges
A	Contemporary sculpture, Rebecca Horn (b.1944)	Body sculptures, drawing and painting machines, sculpture from found objects	Shape and form, creating unusual spaces and places, sculpture you can wear!

Pineapple with Insects, **engraved by J. Mulder, plate 1 from '*The Metamorphosis of the Insects of Surinam*', c.1688–1701 (hand-coloured engraving), Maria Sibylla Graff Merian (1647–1717)**

Media	Intent	Follow-up/Links
Watercolour paintings recreated as engravings (prints) in books for scientists to study.	A scientific study of the plant and insect life of South America from the position of a European visitor, an outsider.	In 1991 artist Damien Hirst (b.1965) created *In and Out of Love*, an exhibition where live butterflies were released in a gallery to stick onto the wet surfaces of newly completed paintings, where they were left to die.
Radical designs with simple modern lines, would not look out of place in a loft apartment today!	Inspired by Japanese designs, especially the decorative black lacquered finishes on traditional Japanese furniture.	See **www.decopix.com.** Many French designers were influenced by Japanese art – they adopted a style called 'Japonisme' at the start of the twentieth century.
Oil paint on canvas, gouache (poster paint) on paper, screenprint	Her interest in optical effects came from her study of Seurat's technique of pointillism.	See **http://nadav.harel.org.il/ Bridget_Riley**, and **www.vasarely. com**. Compare Riley's work to the colourful paintings of Victor Vaserely (1908–97).
Metal, leather, feathers, working machine parts	Action and movement makes art, sometimes by the artist wearing the sculpture, sometimes by a machine on its own.	French artist Yves Klein (1928–62) made paintings by using women's bodies as 'living paintbrushes' rolling across blank canvases, see **www.yveskleinarchives.org/works/ works2_us.html**.

Leather chair with black lacquered frame, c.1930, Eileen Gray (1879–1976)

Women artists and designers II

	Outcome	Subject	Elements
A / **D**	Photography, Cindy Sherman (b.1954)	Self-portraits where she disguises herself as different people.	Lighting and shade, viewpoint and composition, humour
A	Painting, Fiona Rae (b.1963)	Abstract painting with lettering and numbers, patterns and symbols	Colour, texture, movement, contrast and form with a sense of depth and space.
D	Mangaka (female manga artist), Rumiko Takahashi (b.1957)	Storytelling (narrative) with action figures and moral messages.	Strong and vibrant colours, composition, each frame is a work of art in itself.
A	Installation artist, Tracy Emin (b.1963)	Emin has been called a 'confessional' artist: she uses her life experiences as subjects for her work.	Shape, form, space, including real objects.

Today

Untitled, 1982, ektachrome photograph, Cindy Sherman (b.1954)

© Courtesy the artist and Metro Pictures

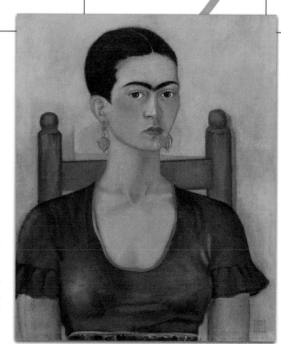

Self-portrait, 1930, oil on canvas, Frida Kahlo (1907–54)

© 2009 Banco de México Diego Rivera & Frida Kahlo Museums Trust. México, D.F./DACS

Media	Intent	Follow-up/Links
Black and white and colour photography, pictures created to look like film stills	Began as a humorous way of creating self-portraits, has developed into a study of identity and how society looks at women in general.	See **www.abcgallery.com/K/kahlo/kahlo.html**. Mexican artist, Frida Kahlo (1907–54) painted personal and telling self-portraits.
Oil and acrylic paint layered onto large-scale canvases with smears, splashes and splatters.	Expressing ideas about the jumbled images of life, energy and excitement. Using influences from fashion, music, comics and the Far East.	Compare Rae's work with the abstract expressionist painters of New York in the 1940s, particularly Franz Kline (1910–62), Willem de Kooning (1904–89) and Sam Francis (1923–94).
Mass-produced printed comic books in Japan are made using recycled paper.	Takahashi is known for using events and scenes from everyday life to create stories of good versus evil.	Riyoko Ikeda-sama (b.1947), 'the mother of manga', began comic strip drawing in the 1960s.
Collecting and constructing mini-environments with a strong personal meaning, making you appreciate what she has experienced herself. Perhaps it helps her 'come to terms' with life by exhibiting it as art.	Her most 'shocking' work was her bed exhibited in 1999.	Beds have been painted by Vincent Van Gogh (1853–90) in 1889, Pablo Picasso (1881–1973) in 1901 and Robert Rauschenberg (1925–2008) in 1955.

Round the World, 1958/9, oil on canvas, Sam Francis (1923–94)

© Samuel L. Francis Foundation/DACS, London 2009

55

Contemporary art, craft and design I

Key: **(A)** Art **(C)** Craft **(D)** Design

	Outcome	Subject	Elements
(A)	Abstract expressionist painting, Mark Rothko (1903–70)	Soft-edged, abstract, colour-field painting, pure painting	Sombre colours, tonal and harmonious, blends and shades, enormous scale
(A) **(D)**	Pop art printing, Andy Warhol (1928–87)	Portraits of stars and icons, items from supermarkets such as soup cans and Coca-Cola bottles.	Repeated patterns of rows and columns, simplified tones, flat areas of colour
(D)	Swinging Sixties and hippie fashion, UK/USA 1960s and 1970s	Union Jack Flags, Ban the Bomb, Love and Peace, Flower Power	Pop- and op-art themes made into everyday fashions, simple black and white and multicoloured patterns.
(A)	Earthworks and Land Art, Robert Smithson (1938–73)	The environment and nature are both the subject and the media for this art form.	Plain and simple shapes and forms recreated in nature on a massive scale.

The 1940s and 50s

25 Coloured Marilyns, **1968, Andy Warhol (1928–87)**

© The Andy Warhol Foundation for the Visual Arts/Artists Rights Society (ARS), NY and DACS, London 2009

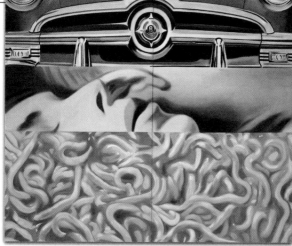

I love you with my Ford, **1961, oil on canvas, James Rosenquist (b.1933)**

© James Rosenquist/DACS, London /VAGA, New York 2009

Media	Intent	Follow-up/Links
Oil paint (used a bit like watercolour), thinned down and built up in washes or layers.	Expressing ideas of calm spirituality.	Artist Jackson Pollock (1912–56) splattered and dripped paint over a canvas stretched on the floor. See him in action at **www.youtube.com/ watch?v=7bICqvmKL5s&NR=1**. Try it yourself at **http://jacksonpollock.org/**.
Silk-screen printing. Warhol also made paintings, sculptures and directed films.	Common objects and experiences made into works of art.	'Everyone is famous for 15 minutes'. David Bowie wrote a song about Warhol, lyrics at **http://david-bowie. co.uk**.
Clothes, shoes, bags, musical instruments, decorated in a hippie way.	Teenagers keen to express themselves differently to their parents and society. Anti-war, Free Love.	Mary Quant (b.1934), **www. maryquant.co.uk**, and Zandra Rhodes (b.1940) **www.zandrarhodes.com**.
Bulldozers and trucks used to move masses of earth and rocks from one place to another.	Art that becomes part of the real-world environment, can be seen from the air or you can walk through and around it.	The spiral form Smithson used is found in nature: pine cones and snail shells, and art: Van Gogh's *Starry Night* (1889).

Spiral Jetty, **1970, Robert Smithson (1938–73)**

© Estate of Robert Smithson/DACS, London/VAGA, New York 2009

Contemporary art, craft and design II

Key: **A** Art **C** Craft **D** Design

	Outcome	Subject	Elements
A **D**	Art Cars, **www. artcars.com**	Transport, cars, motorbikes, vans, buses	Colour and pattern, permanent or temporary decoration, additional shape and forms
D	Contemporary graphic design	Logo (corporate) design, photography, exhibition design, design for print and websites	2-D graphics, slick, high-quality finish, line and colour, balance of lettering and images
A	Contemporary sculpture, Tony Cragg (b.1949)	Abstract forms based on molecules, maps and human figures.	Shape and form, colour and texture, scale and space
A	The White Cube, London, contemporary art gallery	Presenting new works of art to the public	Space, light and atmosphere affect how art is displayed and experienced.

Today

Landscape No. 2,
1964, oil on canvas,
Tom Wesselmann (1931–2004)

© Tom Wesselmann/DACS, London/
VAGA, New York, 2009

Media	Intent	Follow-up/Links
Recycled and found objects, badges, spray paint, stickers	A form of protest, anti-'new car' culture, promoting individuality and imagination, a bit of fun	Cars often feature in artists' work, from Balla's speed-car painting (1913) to Dali's *Rainy Taxi* (1938) to Julian Opie's sculptures and screen-prints (1998).
Most graphics are created using ICT using digital photography and programs like Photoshop.	Marketing and sales, advertising and promotion, image and presentation	Graphic design studios **www.ggs.co.uk**, **www.beyond-design.co.uk** and **www.springdigital.co.uk**.
Complete and broken objects saved from skips and rearranged to make new 2-D and 3-D forms.	By using someone's rubbish to create something new, Cragg makes you think about the life of the planet, its past and, more importantly, its future.	Sculpture really needs to be experienced in real life, pictures in books or on screen don't do it justice. Visit the Cass Foundation to appreciate this, **www.sculpture.org.uk**.
Painters, sculptors, installation and performance artists, photographers and filmmakers	Raises the status of living artists, provocative, controversial, daring	Look at **www.whitecube.com**, then find out more about the artists and their work.

***George and the Dragon*, 1984,
plastic, wood and aluminium,
Tony Cragg (b.1949)**

© Courtesy the artist and Lisson Gallery

Developing your ideas

- Develop your work by making judgements about it as you go along.

- Developing your work and ideas is a skill that should be practised until it becomes second nature.

Development is not just repetition

In GCSE Art and Design terms, to develop something means to change it for the better. This could be by **adding** things – such as details or shading to a drawing – or by **taking away** surplus things – such as fussy flourishes on lettering that make it difficult to read.

- It is important to improve the original piece of work by your thoughts and actions.
- This may be easy enough to grasp when it's applied to something real – a painting or a design for a poster – but it can be hard to develop ideas.

If 'developing' is about 'improving', then it relies on your ability to decide what is good and what is not. You want to keep the good bits – and even make them better! – and do something to change the rest as well.

A third, fourth or even fifth version, developing as you go, is not just repeating what has gone before, it is a process of 'development'.

Different ways of developing your work and ideas

Different people work best in different ways. You must decide for yourself the best way for you to work. Here are some examples:

Cyclical development

A common way to develop ideas is in a **'cyclical'** or **'spiral'** fashion. This is when you work through an idea until you reach the stage where it fizzles out. You then go back a step or two, and pick up the idea again, but this time take it off in a different direction. If that one dries up too, you go back again, and so on.

Creative thinking

Creative thinking is where you take two unrelated ideas and put them together to create one new one. For example, you could merge the ideas of 'insect bodies' and 'human form' and develop the idea of body armour for an ice hockey player based on the colours, shape and textures of beetles.

Using more difficult media

Try out and experiment with **more difficult** techniques and materials.

- In most areas of art, craft and design there are tools, materials and techniques that need more practice to master, but which give much better results in the long run.
- For example, in textiles, you might make a simple pattern on a fabric by stippling fabric paints through a stencil, but you could develop a more complex repeating pattern using a screenprinting process.

The problem with 'inspiration'

A common misconception about art, craft and design is that creative people have to be 'inspired'. Some people call it the **'feel-like factor'**: 'I can't work today, I don't feel like it'. It is probably true that you work better when you do feel like it, but no one can afford the luxury of waiting around until they feel like working!

In order for any self-respecting artist, crafts worker or designer to survive and make a living, they have to be as dedicated, hard-working and disciplined as any other person in any other profession. It is the same for GCSE students!

study hint >>

Whatever approach you take, thinking is best done whilst 'doing'. 'Doing' also helps you to think things out. Work out ideas on the pages of your work journal in words and pictures.

Supporting studies are not just preparatory studies

It is very important to develop your work and ideas during the **preparation period** for the ESA.

- You will need to be disciplined and determined because there is no time to waste between getting the paper and completing the final piece.
- Use all your **preparatory work** to help you to create your final piece under exam conditions.

study hint >>

Take all your preparatory work into the exam room. Lay it out so that you have lots of visual clues to remind you how to do your final piece.

Whaaam!, print

> People who are not artists often feel that artists are inspired. But if you work at your art you don't have time to wait to be inspired.
> **John Cage**

> If you know exactly what you're going to do, what's the good in doing it?
> **Pablo Picasso**

Useful annotations

- Your teachers and examiners know what media you have used, but they don't necessarily know how you felt about using it. This is what annotations can tell them.

- Whatever you write keep it simple and straight to the point. Use notes, key words and phrases, bullet points and references.

What to write, what not to write

- Writing must add to the artwork something you can't show in any other way – it should not just repeat what is there already.
- The most common mistake students make in GCSE Art and Design is labelling – adding headings or labels to something when it's perfectly obvious what it is!
- If you have drawn a picture of a horse in charcoal as part of your study on 'Transport', you could note down why you chose to draw it, how it links with the transport theme, or whether charcoal was a good choice or not.

study hint >>

Don't put obvious labels on your work.

Handwritten or word-processed

Handwritten notes are all that is needed, but make them clear and easy to read. If you have a lot to write, a critique of an artist's or designer's work for example, you can type it on a computer.

study hint >>

It can be effective to print your text on clear acetate so that it can lie on top of pictures on the page.

Decoration or meaning?

Some students develop annotation as part of the artwork itself. The look of the words on the page is as important as their meaning. Many artists, crafts workers and designers include lettering and text within their work to add meaning as well as to decorate the surface. Look at ceramics by Grayson Perry, street art graffiti and paintings by Tom Phillips, Barbara Kruger and Tracey Emin.

A picture paints a thousand words.
Frederick R. Barnard

study hint >>

Only use words when pictures won't do. Build up your artistic vocabulary. It is important to use the right art terms in your writing.

Who is reading?

Writing should add something essential to your artwork. Large amounts of text photocopied from books or downloaded from the Internet are nearly always irrelevant.

- Carefully select a few snippets of information linked to your work.
- Add these, preferably by hand, to your sketches and drawings.

>> **key fact** Just copying and pasting from your secondary source to your work journal tells the examiner nothing about your ability to review, select from and analyse information.

study hint >>

Too much writing can show up a weakness in your determination to improve your art and design skills. It's better to practise your drawing.

Explanation and evaluation

Writing in GCSE Art and Design has two main purposes: explanation and evaluation.

- In **explanation** you **show** and **describe** the thinking behind your work.
- In **evaluation** you make **judgements** about your work and **justify** your opinions with reasons.

study hint >>

All artists, craft workers and designers make notes while they work to explain and justify to others, what they do.

Dos and don'ts of annotation

Artist's life and times

- Do include a few basic facts about the artist, craftworker or designer. Letters and interviews are a useful source of information because they are in the artist's own words.
- Do explain the reasons behind a particular artist's work, if you have similar reasons behind yours.

- Don't give biographical details about an artist's family and where they grew up, unless it helps you to understand where they are coming from.
- Don't list the schools, colleges and universities they went to.
- Don't copy out their CV.

Materials, processes and techniques

- Do say why you did what you did.
- Do say whether the effect was what you expected.
- Do say what have you learnt by doing it, regardless of the result.

- Don't label your work with information that is obvious. The examiners know when you've used oil pastels – you don't need to tell them.
- Don't say what a drawing is of.

A critical vocabulary

Pattern

diamonds	negative	simple
embellish	order	spiral
flowing	ornamental	stamp
fluid	overlap	stencil
geometric	plain	structure
irregular	positive	symmetric
natural	repeat	uniform

Shape

angular	harmonious	profile
body	image	rough-hewn
conical	knead	sculpt
figure	model	sharp
form	mould	silhouette
frame	outline	uniform
geometric	precise	vague

Form and space

advance	motif	scale
angled	natural	scatter
carve	ornament	solid
cast	perspective	stacked
decorate	pointed	structure
depth	proportion	tactile
human	recede	volume
monumental	rounded	woven

Colour

blend	intense	saturated
bright	luminous	secondary
clash	mixed	soft
cold	opaque	tint
deep	pale	translucent
dull	pastel	transparent
glowing	primary	vibrant
harmonious	pure	warm

Line

angular	flowing	scribble
broken	fluent	sweeping
confident	free	tight
faint	hesitant	woolly

Tone

bleach	dark	harsh
bright	fade	intense
contrast	fair	smooth
crisp	gradation	sombre

Composition

background	distant	middle-ground	scale
blurred	eye-line	near	shape
complex	focus	perspective	sharp
confused	foreground	plane	space
design	form	proportion	symmetry

Light

artificial	gentle	natural
dapple	harsh	night
dark	haze	shading
ethereal	highlight	shadow
evening	intense	soft
fall of light	light	source
fierce	midday	tone

Feeling

alive	exciting	lonely
atmospheric	expressive	nostalgic
cheeky	fresh	proud
delicate	humorous	sad
depressing	imposing	shocking
dignified	intimidating	threatening
disturbing	joyous	uplifting

Texture

bobbly	flat	jagged	sharp	splatter
coarse	glaze	matt	shiny	thick
cross-hatching	hatching	rough	smooth	thin
fine	impasto	scumble	soft	wash

Kind of art

abstract	fake	mundane	representational
copied	fantasy	noble	seascape
derivative	figurative	non-representational	sentimental
distorted	impressionistic	pastiche	still life
emotional	impressive	pattern	surreal
exaggerated	interior	portrait	symbolic
exterior	landscape	religious	twee

What is it?

aquatint	ceramic	etching	model	screen print
assemblage	collage	fresco	mural	sculpture
bas-relief	design	gouache	painting	sketch
caricature	diptych	lithograph	photograph	stencil
cartoon	drawing	logo	print	tempera
carving	easel painting	miniature	relief	triptych

It is worth taking a few minutes to remind yourself of a few key facts. An obvious one is that everyone has things they like and things they don't – you do, your teachers do and even the examiners do. If you visit an art gallery with a group of your classmates it is likely that you would all choose different works to study because you get drawn to them for a whole range of different reasons.

In the world of GCSE Art and Design this simple truth leads to difficulties. It would be wrong if your work was judged on whether your teacher or the examiner liked it or not, so a list of the assessment objectives has been devised meaning that your GCSE grade is not left up to the personal opinion of the examiner. See page xi for the four Assessment Objectives (AOs) against which your GCSE work is marked.

If you boil down the AOs into their simplest from you end up with something like the following.

AO1 Thinking up some ideas inspired by different starting points

Just where do you start when given a title, a theme or a topic to work from? Even the 'best' artists have to use some form of research to feed their inspiration.

A few minutes spent reading about any famous artists, craft workers or designers shows that some get their ideas by looking back to the art of previous times, others use inspiration from the wonderful world of nature; some use themes and ideas from stories, poems, music or religion, whilst others use the visual elements of shape, colour and pattern to start from. Whatever they do has to come from somewhere and it is unlikely that it just pops into their head!

You will need to 'feed' your ideas by looking at lots and lots of different art, craft and design – and the more you do the more marks you will get for this AO.

AO2 Making your work better as you do it

Whatever level of skill or ideas you have to start with you will only improve if you push yourself to try something new, risk making a few mistakes and getting it wrong from time to time!

It is the most natural thing in the world of art, craft and design that when you make a mistake you want to tear it up and throw it away – as if every single thing you do is going to be displayed for all to see and you will be ashamed if it's not brilliant.

GCSE is not like that – remember that you are **learning** about art and design and it is important to show **how** you learn as well as **what** you learn. This is what this AO shows.

AO3 Finding and saving primary and secondary sources

This AO links very closely to the first two because it is about the visual forms that you use to record the ideas and inspiration that come from the starting points in AO1 and the skills you use to show them in AO2. Perhaps the most traditional forms of presenting these ideas are drawing and painting, and every GCSE student will have plenty of examples of their drawing and painting skills in their work journals. Nowadays more and more artists use digital photography, film, video, animation, making models and 3-D constructions to record and work out their ideas – you don't have to stick to the usual ways either.

AO4 Drawing this all together into a finished work of art, craft or design

As if all this wasn't enough, you need to pull all your ideas and research together and shape them into a finished piece of work – using the skills you have practised and the knowledge you have gained along the way.

To get the highest marks for this AO you also need to show how everything you did (the process) helped you create your final outcome (the product) and – an area that gets overlooked by some students – how well you were able to achieve what you set out to do: that you had a goal and you didn't lose sight of it.

The next nine pages are helpful writing frames that link directly to the AOs. You should use them to make sure that what you do is on track for GCSE success. They can be used at any time during your course. They could help you put together your portfolio for the controlled assessment; they could be used to help you review what you've done at different stages in a project; or they could be photocopied and stapled together as an 'evaluation' booklet and filled in at the end of the ESA.

Assessment Objective 1

Think up some ideas inspired by looking into different starting points

Name .... **Theme** ....

Some artwork I have researched is good, including ....

....

....

and I think they are good because ....

....

....

Some artwork I researched is not so good, such as ....

....

....

and I think this because ....

....

....

Ideas I found interesting were ....

....

....

I like the skills some artists use to create their work, such as ....

....

....

Some art affects the way you think and feel, examples I discovered were ....

....

....

Assessment Objective 1

List some facts from your research into different cultures

Name .... **Theme** ....

A particular culture I researched for this task is called ....

....

The period of time when this happened was ....

....

and the place in the world where it happened was ....

....

Strong features of this culture are ....

....

....

....

and I can describe the way it looks as ....

....

....

....

....

Ideas from this culture I could use in my own work are ....

....

....

....

....

....

Looking closely at artwork and explaining why you chose it

Name .... **Theme** ....

One particular work of art/craft/design I researched for this task was created by ....

....

....

Title (if it has one) ....

....

Date it was created ....

In this art work I can describe the shapes and forms as ....

....

....

The colours and tones are ....

....

....

and the surface pattern and texture looks and feels like ....

....

....

I chose this artwork because ....

....

....

How I might use it to help me with my own work ....

....

....

Assessment Objective 2

Making your work better as you do it

Name .... **Theme** ....

Some things went well and others went wrong.

Things that went well were ....

....

....

....

....

Things that didn't go as planned were ....

....

....

....

....

I have learned to look closely at my work as I do it and this helps me to improve.

One example of how I improved it would be ....

....

....

Also, some of my art skills have got better, these are ....

....

....

There may be some room for improvement though, and I could make my work

even better by ....

....

....

Practise your skills and try new ones

Name .... **Theme** ....

Dry media I have used in my art studies for this project are ....

....

These are good for ....

....

and not so good for ....

....

Wet media I have used in my art studies for this project are ....

....

These are good for ....

....

and not so good for ....

....

Other media I have used in my art studies for this project ....

....

These are good for ....

....

and not so good for ....

....

Using these different media has helped me decide what is best for my project ....

....

....

....

Assessment Objective 3

Find and save useful (secondary) art and design sources

Name .... **Theme** ....

I researched my theme by finding pictures of ....

....

....

....

Ideas I've had that were inspired by this research are ....

....

....

....

Some things I have learned when doing this work are ....

....

....

....

It was useful to do this, because ....

....

....

....

....

WRITING FRAME 3/2

Recording things from primary sources

Name .... **Theme** ....

Real life objects I chose to record for my work are ....

....

....

I recorded them in the following ways ....

....

....

....

I chose these because ....

....

....

....

and some ideas I've had inspired by this are ....

....

....

....

I improved my work as I did it by ....

....

....

....

Some things I learned by doing this are ....

....

....

Assessment Objective 4

Show off your skills by creating your own individual work of art, craft or design

Name .... **Theme** ....

Here is a description of my final outcome ....

....

....

The subject matter is ....

....

....

I can describe the visual elements ....

....

the colours and tones are ....

....

lines and shapes I used are ....

....

and pattern and texture can be seen in ....

....

Things I changed as I worked on it were ....

....

My intention with this work is to show ....

....

Overall I am pleased / not pleased with my work because ....

....

If I could do it again, I might do things differently, these would be ....

....

Review your work and explain how your research affected your final outcome

Name .... **Theme** ....

Some things I changed as I worked on my final piece were ....

....

....

....

....

Some links I made with other artists work were ....

....

....

....

....

Overall I am pleased / not pleased with my finished piece of work because ....

....

....

....

....

If I could do it again, I might do things differently, these would be ....

....

....

....

....

If I were to give my work a title it would be ....

....

Starting points

- After you've read through the exam paper, use the information to help you get started straight away.

- Spider diagrams can help you to come up with a range of ideas: use pictures as well as words.

GCSE Art and Design exam questions

There are no right answers to GCSE Art and Design exam questions because the exam papers don't even include questions!

- Unlike other subjects, in art and design it is pointless trying to work out what the examiner wants.
- Be brave and take risks.

Use what you're given to best effect

Examiners put time and effort into making papers that give you the best chance of success.

- You may have a single theme for your exam, or a series of topics to choose from.
- Whichever it is, you must read through the paper fully and use any **clues** left there by the examiners to help you.
- For example, if there is a list of artists, websites or art books, see if they trigger some ideas.
- Often examiners will include details in the questions designed specifically to give you a **direction** to go in.
- For example, on the theme of 'Water', if the paper lists 'reflections, waves, ripple, splash, floating, flow and movement', these are **starting points** about the way water looks, moves and feels: a **visual and tactile** response to water.
- If the paper lists 'dockside accident, surfs up!, storm at sea, "abandon ship", beach landing or round-the-world challenge', the examiner is suggesting a **narrative response**: dramatic events that occur in and around the sea.

study hint >>

The exam paper is only a starting point. Examiners are best pleased when they see work inspired by the question paper that they could not have predicted.

study hint >>

Try to see if you can spot any 'hints' in the way the papers are worded.

Just a Wire Away, acrylic on three canvases

Mind-mapping techniques, brainstorming and spider diagrams

Put together your ideas on a new theme by drawing out a **spider diagram**.

- Put the title or **topic** in the centre of the page and draw lines outwards from this linking up with associated ideas, or **subthemes**, as they occur.
- Some students find this liberating: it allows them to dream up ideas and alternative approaches that they wouldn't have considered.
- It is a good idea to use pictures as well as words. Otherwise you can simply end up with a long list of words.

A slightly more focused mind-mapping technique is to write down the theme and then divide the area around your theme into three sections:

- Primary Observation,
- Ideas and Emotions
- Media and Techniques.

Try to come up with sub-themes that fit these categories.
Here is an example with the theme 'Townscape':

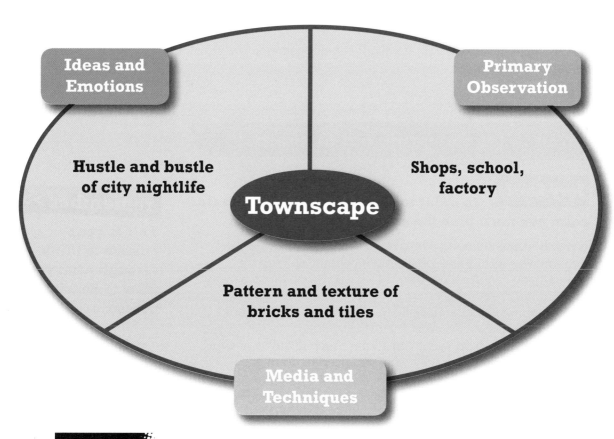

>> **key fact** This approach helps to speed up the time between being given a theme and actually starting your work. Whichever approach to art, craft and design work you prefer – whether you think you are an 'ideas', 'observation' or 'materials' person – this **brainstorming** can get you going quickly and with enthusiasm.

The exam days

 Ten hours goes much quicker than you expect.

 What is meant by 'your own unaided work'.

The '60-Minute Makeover' effect

You may have a chance to start and finish a piece of artwork in one go in your trial GCSE exam in December, or possibly January, of Year 11.

- Sometimes the trial exam is spread over several lessons and doesn't have the feeling of an 'exam' about it.
- The real thing, starting and finishing a piece of work, virtually from scratch, in two five-hour days is a very different experience.
- When you start it seems like you have all the time in the world stretching ahead of you, but by the end of the first day, when you should be half-way through, you might begin to experience the '60-Minute Makeover' effect if you haven't planned properly.
- Like in the TV house decorating programme, you start to panic, thinking you won't be finished in time. This leads to mistakes which makes you even more anxious, which leads to more errors and so on.
- Hopefully, again just like on TV, it will all come together and you will end up with the result you hoped for!

Planning takes the panic out of exams!

>> **key fact** In order to stay in control and remain calm you must plan the exam days.

- One way is to use the normal breaks as 'markers'.
- In the same way as morning break and lunchtime split up the school day, you can use these breaks to keep you on target as you work.
- Use the planning frame on page 80 to map out what you should have done by when.
- This frame will only help you if you add as much detail as possible.
- Be specific and describe exactly what you need to do in each period of the exam days.

remember >>

This is your chance to think through what you want to do without pressure.

GCSE Art and Design exam rules and regulations

Your own unaided work

- As in all exams, the work you do in your GCSE Art and Design exam must be entirely your own and unaided effort.
- You must make all the decisions about your work yourself and, of course, all the practical work must be done by you.

No talking

- You must not communicate with any other candidate during the exam.
- It is against the rules to ask for anyone's help or to give them advice about their work.
- Even if you are not talking about the work, you are likely to disturb someone's concentration.

Invigilation and specialist help

- Normally, your exam will be invigilated by an art and design teacher, because there are some things that only a specialist teacher can help with.
- If, for example, a water pot spills and a candidate's work is at risk of being spoilt, an experienced art and design teacher can help to minimise the damage and get the candidate back to work quickly.
- The exam regulations allow an art and design teacher to help if a candidate has a technical problem that needs specialist or expert advice, when their help doesn't affect the 'artistic' quality of the final piece. This would include advice on the best glue to use to fix two materials together.

study hint >>

Don't wait until the exam days to make a piece of work in a new material, or in a new style that you haven't worked out beforehand. All too often this ends in disaster!

Planning for your exam writing frame

Here is a writing frame to help you plan out your work over the ten hour period.

Name	Tutor group	Art option group	Art teacher

Title:

Complete the following boxes IN FULL

What I have chosen to do for my final piece is

This will show the exam theme of '   ' by

Artists/designers I have researched for my exam are

Primary research work completed in my work journal BEFORE the exam includes

Secondary research work completed in my work journal BEFORE the exam includes

Planning for the 'TEN HOUR EXAM'

On Day 1 (DATE   ) I plan to

By lunchtime I will have

In the afternoon I will

On Day 2 (DATE _____) I plan to _____

By lunchtime I will have _____

In the afternoon I will _____

Signed _____ Date _____

Here is an example of a completed writing frame a GCSE student used to help them achieve success in the ten hour period ... and it worked!

Name	Tutor group	Art option group	Art teacher

Reflections

Complete the following boxes IN FULL

What I have chosen to do for my final piece is *a sculpture of a chrome tap with a drip of water coming out of it, and a picture of a cat reflected in the water.*

This will show the exam theme of '**Reflections**' by *the tap's chrome surface and the reflection of the cat's face in the water – I will also varnish my sculpture so that the whole thing is reflective.*

Artists/designers I have researched for my exam are *mainly M C Escher, but also Monet's water lily pictures for the water reflections. I also looked at David Hockney's swimming-pool pictures and sculptors like Claes Oldenburg for the way they made sculptures of everyday objects.*

Primary research work completed in my work journal BEFORE the exam includes *drawing taps from lots of different angles to get the scale and the shape right. I also tried drawing water as it dripped from the tap, but this was too hard. I drew my pet cat using chalk pastels and tried painting it as well.*

Secondary research work completed in my work journal BEFORE the exam includes *copying M C Escher's eye and water pictures. I also found some pictures of taps from a DIY catalogue – drawing these helped me get the effect of chrome on my tap. It was easier to draw chrome from a photo because the reflection didn't keep changing.*

Planning for the 'TEN HOUR EXAM'

On Day 1 (DATE   ) I plan to *have the form of my sculpture finished ready for painting.*

By lunchtime I will have *made the framework and fixed chicken wire on it with wire and staples, forming the shape of the tap and the drop.*

In the afternoon I will *cover it with Mod Roc and, if there's time, paint it all over with white emulsion paint so that it's ready for painting tomorrow.*

On Day 2 (DATE   ) I plan to *paint the details on my sculpture, copying them from my work journal. I shall use acrylic paint and varnish the whole thing with PVA glue for a shiny and reflective finish.*

By lunchtime I will *have painted the light and shade, and the chrome effects on the tap.*

In the afternoon I will *go on to paint the cat's reflection.*

Signed _____ Date _____

Exam-day essentials

1 Take all your preparation work into the exam with you.

2 Artists surround themselves with pictures and objects that interest and inspire them. Bring some things that stimulate ideas and approaches in you.

3 Check out the art materials and equipment that will be available to you on the day. Don't wait until the last minute to discover that another candidate wants to use the same piece of equipment as you!

4 Bring in any special or unusual materials or resources. If you're planning on using something a little out of the ordinary, ask your teacher if it's available in school. If not, find out where you can get it and bring it in yourself, having practised with it first in your work journal.

Equipment and materials list

1 Go back through your work journal, looking at the preparation you have done. Make a note about the media and equipment you have used. What worked best? What do you need to complete your final piece?

2 Reserve a page in your work journal to list everything you're likely to need for your exam.

   The list should include:

   • the ground or support to work on, or the framework on which to build;

   • drawing materials: pencils, charcoal, pastels;

   • colour media: paints, inks, dyes, glazes;

   • tools and equipment: different sizes and types of brush, scissors and rulers, clay tools and batik pots, printing presses, sewing machines and computers;

   • joining and fixing: glue, staples, tape, thread;

   • 3-D media: clay, wood, plastic, metal;

   • fabrics and textiles;

   • any other specialist or unusual materials: photographic paper and chemicals, metallic paints, fabric transfer paper for the inkjet printer.

> **study hint >>**
>
> Don't forget to include on your materials list anything you need to mount and present your final piece. Think about how to show your work when it's finished.

Achieving a high-quality outcome

 'High quality' means that every part is the best it can possibly be.

 Your outcome should follow on naturally from your preparation.

Simple rules to help you make a success of your exam

- Have all your materials ready at the start.
- Organise your workspace and keep it tidy.
- Have your exam plan to hand and refer to it regularly.
- Keep an eye on the time.

study hint >>

You must think of your work as a complete piece and not just as its different parts.

2-D ways of working

Pace and review

- Work at a pace that not only allows you to use all the time to best effect, but also allows you to stop briefly every now and then to make sure that you are happy with your work. Does it show off what you can do?
- Don't focus so closely on a small part of your work that it fails to come together as a whole. Even if the eyes on a face you are painting are brilliantly drawn, if the rest of the proportions are not right, the composition will not work.
- Paint your picture from back to front and from top to bottom. It is a mistake to do the most 'important' part first.

Solitary, oil pastel

3-D ways of working

With 3-D work, the size and scale are very important, as are the many technical concerns with the materials you might be using.

- Make a **'maquette'** first. This is a small-scale model, often using the same materials as the final piece.
- If your plans are large scale, a stage-set design for example, make a **'proposal'** for a final piece. This is a model of what the final piece would look like if it were actually made.

study hint >>

Find examples of graded work from last year's exam to see the standard.

Wraps. mixed media

When the exam is over

 When the exam is over it is important to show that you can look back and identify the things that went well and those that didn't. This is in two parts: 1) evaluating as you go; 2) looking back over your work – a critical review

 Keep it short, sharp and to the point.

Evaluating as you go

Evaluation is generally thought of as something done at the end of a process – making an **assessment** or **judgement** about the quality of the work completed.

- But evaluation is just as much **part of the process** of making art as it is a summing-up.
- Every little choice or decision you make comes about as a result of how well you think your work is going.
- What you need to do is to make these judgements clear.

study hint >>
Evaluation is not just a summary of what you did – the examiner should be able see this in your journal.

Looking back – critical review

Why evaluate your work? GCSE examiners need your own honest **review** of your work to help them **assess** how well you have **understood** the process you've been through.

- What they don't need is a step-by-step description of what you did.

Ask your parents or guardians, brothers and sisters, classmates or, better still, students who are not taking GCSE Art and Design for their opinion of your work.

- Try explaining to them how and why your work is the way it is.

study hint >>
See list of dos and don'ts for evaluation on pages 86–7.

study hint >>
Use the word banks on pages 64–5 and pages 90–102 to help you evaluate your work.

study hint >>
Get a second opinion.

>> **key fact** If you can find the words you need to explain your work to them, you will find the words you need to evaluate your work for the examiner.

Keep it short, sharp and to the point

Writing should not take over from the visual aspect of the GCSE.

- If you find that you are doing more writing than drawing or painting, you are probably doing too much.
- Written evaluations in notes or short sentences are all that you need to do.
- No essays please!

Self-assessment questions

My personal response

1 Imagination	• Have I thought of some new ideas?
2 Originality	• Have I done it before? • Has anyone done it before? • Have I added my own style to it?
3 Sensitivity and quality	• Did I make good choices? • How well have I used the materials I chose? • Is it good? • Would I like to show it off?
4 Understanding	• Does my work look as if it makes sense? • If necessary, could I explain it to a stranger?
5 Progress	• Have I done better than last time?

study hint >>

Some of these questions can be answered with a simple 'yes' or 'no', but most need brief descriptions. More can be learnt by adding 'how', 'why' or 'where' after these questions.

The art-making process

1 Organisation	• Did I organise myself well? • Did I use all the available time constructively?
2 Observation	• Have I used my eyes to study and observe?
3 Research	• How much effort have I made to find reference material?
4 Experiment	• How many different ideas, materials and techniques did I use?
5 Neatness	• Have I worked carefully and tidily?

The finished piece or outcome

1 Pattern and texture	• Are the surfaces (whether drawn or real) lively and varied?
2 Colour	• Have I used colour to good effect? • Did I choose shades and tints carefully? • Do I know how to get the colour I want?
3 Line and tone	• Are the lines clear or hidden? • Have I used a range of tones, from lightest to darkest?
4 Shape, form and space	• Are the shapes accurate? • Where necessary, does my work look 3-D? • Is my work organised how I want it?

Saying 'why' and not just 'what'

- The dos and don'ts of evaluation.

- Phrases to use and some to avoid.

- Make sure you evaluate the right things by referring back to the assessment objectives.

study hint >>

This section includes sample phrases used by GCSE students to evaluate their work. They are not here for you to copy, but you may be able to adapt them to fit your own experience.

AO1: Starting points

Do use phrases like	Don't use phrases like
• When I started out I wanted to … and so I began by collecting … • As my collection grew my idea changed from … to … • When I looked really closely at work by … I discovered that • I chose to draw … because they fitted in with my theme by … • I think my observation skills have improved as I have worked on this … because I have managed to create a better sense of 3-D form than I have in the past.	• Here are some pictures I have collected from magazines and off the Internet. *(Say why you chose them. What did you do with the ones you haven't used?)* • This is a drawing of … I have done using … , and I am quite pleased with it. *(Doesn't say why you chose the particular object or media. What do you think is good about it?)* • I studied this picture and then did a version of my own in pencil. *(Why?)*

AO2: Making your work better

Do use phrases like	Don't use phrases like
• The artist has used lines and shapes that are rhythmical and wavy. The picture is of a flower, a natural object. The wavy lines remind me of water flowing in a river, which is also natural. • … inspired me a lot. I particularly like the way he distorted people's faces, so I made a distorted picture of him. • I like the work of … He used clouds to create a dreamy, floating feeling. I have drawn objects changing into other objects like in dreams.	• There are many different types of art form, here I have picked out some that I found. *(This phrase is only a heading. Describe the art forms you have chosen, in colours, textures, patterns and shapes.)* • … was the most sophisticated of the major pop artists in terms of his astute analysis of visual convention and his ironic exploitation of past styles. *(This is obviously copied from somewhere. Explain it in your own words.)*

AO3: Primary and secondary sources

Do use phrases like	Don't use phrases like
• One idea I had was to … As I worked on it, another idea I had was … This in turn led me to think of … Finally, I put two of these ideas together and got … • At the start, I found it very hard to draw because … but, after I had practised with *'media'* my drawing improved and became … • By using *'media'* in this way, I managed to create the effect of a rough, and textured surface that goes well with my theme. I experimented by adding *'another medium'* but this was difficult to work with and the effect was lost.	• I used different media to create different effects. *(Be specific and explain what effects were created by which media.)*

AO4: Making links between your work and research

Do use phrases like	Don't use phrases like
• I think my final piece is successful because … • I am pleased with the way my final piece came out because … • As I worked on my final piece I discovered that … and so I used this to help me achieve a better effect.	• If I had more time I would have done it better. *(This phrase is actually saying 'I didn't use the preparation period properly to plan out my final piece!')* • I think my final piece is quite good and I'm quite pleased with it. *(This is a very lukewarm comment. Does your work have an equal amount of good bits and not so good bits?)*

study hint >>

Draw a line across two pages in your work journal: 'Strengths' written at one end and 'Weaknesses' at the other. Place descriptions of your work along this line and explain why you placed them there.

Dance, coloured pencil on canvas

Student checklist

A form to help you keep track of your work

Candidate name	Candidate number

Work journal	✔	Notes
Present		
Sketchbook form		
Loose sheet/Other		
Research and experiment		
Annotation and evaluation		

Research/Record	✔	Notes
Present		
Primary research		
Secondary research		
Imaginative response		
Range of ideas		
Select and organise		

Analyse/Evaluate	✔	Notes
Historical references		
Contextual references		
Real works of art		
Other cultures		
Specialist vocabulary		
Value judgements		
Critical verbal/written		
Critical visual		
Bibliography/refs		

Develop ideas	✔	Notes
Show a range of ideas		
Sustain investigations		
Make inventive links		
Develop skills		

Displaying your work

- Do include examples of direct observational and primary research.
- Do include work using different media and techniques.
- Do include all sketchbooks and work journals.
- Do use real or imaginary horizontal and vertical lines to arrange your work.
- Do use dressmaker pins or staples put in at an angle. If you have to use drawing pins, match the head to the colour of the mount.

- Don't cut around drawings using scissors. Always use a trimmer.
- Don't double mount your work. Be as neat and precise as possible.
- Don't use too much glue, a small dab on each corner is enough.
- Don't decorate your work unnecessarily. Keep it simple.

Mounting your work

- Black border: pencil drawings on white paper.
- Border cream, grey or beige: brightly coloured paintings.
- Bright coloured border: emphasise elements of the picture.

Samples of layouts

	Using horizontals and verticals. Make the gaps work as well.	✔
	'Washing line': all pictures 'hang' from an imaginary line. Also works with a strong vertical line.	✔
	'Horizon': all pictures are placed above or below an imaginary horizontal line. Also works with an imaginary vertical line.	✔
	Chaos: nothing relates to anything else - looks untidy and doesn't make you want to look at it.	✘

Glossaries and word banks

 These pages include glossaries of different terms you should be familiar with. These are organised under three separate headings:

1 **Knowledge of art and artists**: what you need to know at GCSE level.

2 **Understanding GCSE art and assessment**: knowing how your work is assessed.

3 **Art, craft and design media and skills**: terms that artists, craftworkers and designers use when talking about their work.

Knowledge of art and artists

This is a list of terms that broadly covers art, craft and design at GCSE level. You may not know much about all of these terms, but you should know something about some of them, and show this in your work.

Term	Description
Aboriginal art	Art made by the native peoples of Australia, whose art is often based on 'dreaming' and 'journeys' and made by creating images with dots of earthy colours. Subjects include the landscape (as seen from above), rivers, mountains, lizards, serpents and other animals and birds.
abstract art	Art that is not representational or realistic, where the visual elements of art (colour, line, tone and shape and so on) are the subject rather than a representation of a person, object or scene.
abstract expressionism	A movement in painting, originating in New York City in the 1940s. It emphasised personal expression and the act of painting itself. Mark Rothko, Jackson Pollock, Willem de Kooning and Franz Kline are abstract expressionists.
art deco	A design style of the 1920s and 1930s where high-quality household and commercial items were made using industrial materials and techniques.
art movement	A group of artists with a common idea and working in a similar style; a convenient way of labelling a style of art. Sometimes called an '-ism', where the style of art is given a name and the ending '-ism' added to it, as Impression*ism* and surreal*ism*. Artists who paint in the style of Impressionism are called Impressionists.
art nouveau	A highly decorative art movement of the late nineteenth century using twisting and twirling plant forms. Gustave Klimt worked in an art nouveau style.
avant-garde	French word meaning 'at the front', used to describe new and often experimental art forms.
baroque	European painting in the seventeenth and early eighteenth centuries, with strong emotional content, dramatic lighting and colour. Caravaggio and Peter Paul Rubens were important baroque artists.
Bauhaus	Famous twentieth century art, craft and design school in Germany dedicated to bringing together artists (such as Paul Klee) with architects and craftworkers.
classicism	Ancient Greek and Roman art that emphasised harmony, proportion and balance. Today it means something based on long-standing standards of style and beauty or, simply, perfection.

Term	Description
conceptual art	A movement of the 1960s and 1970s where the artistic idea is more important than a painting or a sculpture. Conceptual artists include Sol LeWitt, Richard Long, Keith Arnatt and Joseph Kosuth.
cubism	An art movement begun by Pablo Picasso and Georges Braque in the early twentieth century in which different sides of an object are shown at the same time.
Dadaism	An anti-art movement around the 1920s that protested against all art that had gone before. Artists staged 'happenings' and one, Marcel Duchamp, even made a sculpture from a urinal. Hans Arp and Max Ernst were Dadaists.
de Stijl	('The style'.) A Dutch art, design and architecture school formed in 1913 by Theo van Doesburg and Piet Mondrian promoting the use of simple geometric shapes and primary colours.
earth art	Huge ambitious artworks of the 1960s created in the environment, which were then photographed to exhibit. Robert Smithson's *Spiral Jetty* in Great Salt Lake is the best-known example.
environmental art	Art on an architectural scale. Where artists create whole environments that can be experienced. Best-known are Christo's 'wrappings projects'.
expressionism	Art that uses distorted shapes and extreme colours to express moods. Developed in and around Germany (1905–25). Artists such as Wassily Kandinsky, Georges Rouault, Oscar Kokoschka, Edvard Munch and Egon Schiele painted in this manner.
fauvism	From the French word 'fauve', meaning 'wild beast'. A style adopted by artists André Derain, Raoul Dufy and Henri Matisse around 1905–10. They painted with loose brushstrokes using strong colours, like a cheerful version of expressionism!
figurative art	Art that is representational with subjects such as people, animals or objects you can easily recognise, although it might not be *realistic*, if the artist has decided to distort or exaggerate parts. The opposite of abstract art.
Futurism	In 1910 an Italian group of artists created work that expressed the movement and energy of bustling life in a modern city. Giacomo Ball, Gino Severini and Umberto Boccioni were Futurists.
Gothic	Gothic architecture and sculpture began in France at the start of the thirteenth century, followed by Gothic painting. The artworks are more graceful, elegant in style and naturalistic than previous forms.
Impressionism	As well as being a French art movement from around 1880, this now means a style of painting in its own right. Mostly painting out of doors, impressionist artists aim to capture the fleeting effects of light and colour in a moment of time. Claude Monet, Berthe Morisot, Pierre-Auguste Renoir and Camille Pissarro are Impressionists.
kinetic art	Sculpture with parts that move either by air or hand or by mechanical power. The best-known kinetic sculptors are Alexander Calder and Jean Tinguely, who specialised in making machines that destroyed themselves!
minimalism	In the USA in the late 1950s, a movement, especially in sculpture, started that aimed to reduce art objects to their bare minimum – the simplest, purest unit that could express the artist's intention. Robert Morris, Carl Andre and Donald Judd developed work that led to the conceptual art movement.
modern art	There is no clear definition of 'modern art'. In the popular press it tends to mean shocking or controversial art that looks simple and easy to do. People often use 'modern art' to mean abstract art that is not easy to understand at first glance. Art critics think that art became 'modern' when artists began making artwork to please themselves and not for a rich or religious patron.

Term	Description
naive art	A term used to describe paintings that are childlike in style, bold in colour and that quite often have a strange sense of perspective. The artists might not be professionally trained. Henri Rousseau, Alfred Wallis and L.S. Lowry worked in this style.
op art	Short for 'optical art', an abstract movement in Europe and the USA, started in the mid-1950s and based on the effects of optical patterns on the brain. Bridget Riley, Victor Vasarely and Joseph Albers worked in this style.
photorealism	Originally meaning 'Art that is more realistic than photographs'. This began in the USA and UK in the late 1960s. The subject matter, usually a figure or everyday scene, is portrayed in an extremely detailed, exacting style. It is also called hyperrealism or superrealism, especially when referring to sculpture. Artists are Richard Estes, Duane Hanson and Chuck Close in the USA, and Malcolm Morley in the UK.
pointillism	Also called 'divisionism'. This is a method of painting developed by Georges Seurat and Paul Signac in the 1880s. They painted scenes using tiny dabs of pure colour that appear to blend together and form different colours when looked at from a distance.
pop art	A movement that began in the UK in the 1950s and that was enthusiastically taken up in the USA during the 1960s. It used the images and techniques of magazines and comics, advertising and popular culture, often in a 'tongue-in-cheek' way. Key British pop artists were Richard Hamilton, Peter Blake and Eduardo Paolozzi, and in the USA the major artists were Andy Warhol, Roy Lichtenstein, James Rosenquist and Claes Oldenburg.
post-Impressionism	Originally this referred to a group of late nineteenth-century painters, including Paul Cezanne, Vincent Van Gogh and Paul Gauguin, who were dissatisfied with expressionism. It is also used to describe artists who take the ideas of Impressionism further.
Pre-Raphaelite Brotherhood	A group of English painters formed in 1848. Dante Gabriel Rossetti was a founding member. Others included Ford Madox Brown, John Everett Millais and William Holman Hunt. They attempted to recapture a style of painting from before the Renaissance, painting from nature, producing detailed, colourful works.
realism	As a general term in art this means representing reality, the opposite of abstract art. In the nineteenth century, especially in France, it was used to describe artists, such as Honoré Daumier, Jean-François Millet and Gustave Courbet, who painted ordinary everyday subjects like country folk at work.
Renaissance	Meaning 'rebirth' in French, this refers to European art between 1400 and 1600. The Renaissance began in Italy with the revival of classical Greek and Roman art and sculpture. Leonardo da Vinci, Michelangelo and Raphael painted realistic representations of space based on strict rules of perspective, and secular subjects as well as religious ones. The High Renaissance period (c.1495–1520) is thought to represent perfection in terms of balance and harmony of proportion.
romanticism	A European art movement of the late eighteenth to mid-nineteenth century. The subjects chosen by romantic artists are always dramatic and painted with feeling, in brilliant colours. Eugène Delacroix, Théodore Géricault, J.M.W. Turner and William Blake were all romantic artists but worked in very different styles.
suprematism	A Russian abstract movement originated by Kasimir Malevich around 1913. He painted flat geometric shapes on plain backgrounds in his attempt to create a pure art that expressed his spiritual feelings.
surrealism	Art movement of the 1920s and 1930s that began with Dadaism in Paris. Surrealists explored the unconscious mind and often painted images from dreams. They also used 'automatic' drawing techniques where doodles were turned into paintings. Surrealist sculptures were made by putting unusual objects together in bizarre ways. René Magritte, Salvador Dali and Joan Miró were surrealists.

Understanding GCSE art and assessment

This is a list of the concepts and ideas about GCSE and art, craft and design that you need to understand to meet the assessment requirements.

Term	Description
aesthetic	'Rightness' or 'perfection', the 'impossible to explain' quality that makes a work of art special to you. This is to do with personal taste and what is particularly beautiful to you, but also connects with some generally held ideas that the majority of people feel.
annotation	Adding words, phrases and notes to your work, especially in your work journal, that explain your thoughts.
analysis	Looking beyond the surface of something and making judgements about what you find out.
art process	Everything you do on the way to producing a finished piece of artwork. The process is as important as the final outcome in GCSE Art and Design.
Assessment Objectives	The statements issued by the QCA that describe what your work will be marked on.
awarding body	Used to be called 'examining board': an organisation that sets, marks and awards GCSEs.
component marking	Marks are given for different components, or parts, of the GCSE course – coursework and the ESA. You need to complete both components.
context	The setting or background for works of art, craft and design.
coursework/units of coursework	All work produced by you during your course up until the ESA. A unit of coursework is a set of work on a theme, or work developed from learning a particular art technique or process.
criticism	The reasons and values used to make judgements about artwork, your own as well as that of others.
evidence	Everything you do that is presented for assessment and that shows how you meet the assessment objectives.
evaluate, evaluation	Making judgements about artwork, your own as well as that of others.
Externally Set Assignment (ESA)	Two-part exam set by the awarding body. You must complete preparation work and a final outcome.
final outcome	Final piece of work completed in a limited time.
to justify	To explain your likes and dislikes by giving reasons.
levels of achievement	A system of progression from low to high, used to describe a candidate's ability. These are: • **limited** – a candidate who doesn't know much about art and has weak art skills. • **basic** – a candidate who knows something about art and is OK at some art practices. • **competent** – a candidate who knows quite a lot about art and shows this in their work, which is reasonably well done. • **confident** – a candidate who knows quite a lot about art and has good art skills, or possibly one who knows a great deal but has weaker art skills. • **fluent** – a candidate who combines what they know and understand about art with good examples of their own work, skilfully done.

Term	Description
moderation	Teachers and examiners getting together to check that their marking is to the same standard.
modify	Making choices and changing your work for the better.
refine	Improving the quality of your work, especially the final outcome.
review	Looking back over your work and picking out the parts that worked well and the parts that didn't.
self-assessment	Making judgements about the strengths and weaknesses of your own work.
visual language	This is made up from the visual (or basic) elements and principles (or rules).
visual elements	The smallest units that art is made from: • **line** – outlines, sketches, doodles or hatching • **tone** – shading from dark to light (sometimes called 'value') • **colour** – everything that isn't black or white! • **pattern** – repeated shapes whether found in nature or man-made • **texture** – how surfaces look or actually feel • **shape** – regular (as in geometric) or irregular (as in nature) • **form** – three-dimensionality, either in appearance or reality • **space** – real or apparent depth and distance.
visual principles	Rules for using the elements. • **harmony** – making sure the elements you use 'accord' with each other • **balance** – not necessarily symmetrical, but always well matched • **scale and proportion** – the size of the work and of the elements in it • **contrast** – giving some elements more impact than others • **rhythm and motion** – the movement of the eye across and around the work • **composition** – arranging the elements into a successful conclusion.
weighting	Where different parts of the GCSE are worth different amounts. In GCSE Art and Design, coursework is worth 60 per cent of the marks and the ESA is worth 40 per cent.
work journal	Sketchbook that shows your working processes and the thinking behind them.

Art, craft and design media and skills

This is a list of terms that have a special meaning when used in art, craft and design. The same words might have slightly different meanings in other contexts.

Term	Description
aerial (or atmospheric) perspective	Changing the tone and colour of things to make them look far away.
acrylic paint	Paint that can be used thickly like oil paint and thinly for transparent watercolour-style washes. Slightly glossy finish, waterproof when dry.
allegory	A painting with hidden meanings, where the subject matter goes beyond what is actually shown.
anatomy	The bones and muscles of the human body, which have always featured in the training programmes of artists and sculptors.
aquarelle	Painting which uses watercolour washes, or a drawing using watercolour pencils.
armature	Metal framework, usually wire, used by sculptors as a skeleton on which to model clay.
artist's proof	A print made by an artist for personal use, signed with A/P and not usually sold.
assemblage	Sculpture made up by putting ready-made or natural objects together.
asymmetric	Not symmetrical, a composition or pattern where the two halves are not the same.
block printing	Printmaking process using carved blocks of wood, metal or lino.
broken colour	Technique of painting by using small brushstrokes that blend when viewed at a distance.
bronze	Metal used for sculpture. Nowadays also means a cast made of bronze.
brushwork	Style of painting used by an artist as their 'signature'.
bust	A sculpture which is a portrait of the head and shoulders of a person.
calligraphy	The art of fine handwriting or lettering. In China and Japan it is as important as painting.
canvas	Coarse fabric such as linen or cotton on which an artist makes a painting. The fabric is first stretched and then primed. Today, artists can buy 'pre-stretched'.
cartoon	A full-size drawing for a wall painting or tapestry. Today, the word means a comic drawing, perhaps with a caption.
catalogue	A list of works of art, includes the artists, the media used and a description the works.
chalk	Soft limestone drawing material.
charcoal	Soft, dark sticks of charred wood (willow or vine) used for drawing.
chiaroscuro	Italian word for 'light–shade' and means using strong contrasts of light and shade to create a sense of 3-D form in a painting.
collage	Originally from the French meaning 'to paste'. Used to describe an artwork made from materials (such as paper or cloth) stuck onto paper or canvas.

Term	Description
colour	Has three basic attributes: hue, intensity and value. • **Hue** – how strong a colour is, its redness, or blueness and so on. • **Saturation, intensity or brilliance** – how bright or dull a colour is. • **Value or tone** – how light or dark a colour is; a lighter colour is called a tint and a darker one, a shade.
colour wheel	The colours of the spectrum arranged in a circle, with complementary colours opposite each other.
colour separation	In printing, the process of making separate plates, stencils or blocks for each colour you intend to print.
complementary colour	Opposite colours on the colour wheel: blue/orange, red/green, yellow/purple.
composition	Organisation of the different elements in a work of art.
copy	Remaking a work of art. Not the same as a fake (which pretends to be the original), a pastiche (which is in the style of the original) or a transcription (which is a copy in a different medium).
cropping	Trimming a picture down to make a better composition.
cross-hatching	Shading using lines criss-crossing each other; closer lines make darker tones.
diptych	Painting, usually an altarpiece, made up of two hinged panels.
drawing	Mark-making, usually with an emphasis on line. Sometimes preparation towards a finished outcome, sometimes a finished work in itself.
earth colours	Natural pigments made from earth such as ochres (yellows) and umbers (browns).
easel	Upright stand used by artists to hold the canvas or panel.
edition	A series of prints made from a printing plate and presented as a numbered set.
egg tempera	Powdered pigment bound together with egg yolk, the first 'liquid' paint.
engraving	Printmaking process where lines are cut in a wood block or scribed onto a metal plate. Engravings can be works of art (where the artist is the engraver) or copies of pre-existing works of art.
etching	Printmaking process that uses acid to create an image on a metal plate. This technique was used in the seventeenth century by Rembrandt, and it is still used today. 'Etching' describes both the process and the outcome.
eye level	An imaginary line level with the *artist's* eye.
fake	A copy of a work of art pretending to be the original.
fine art	The practice of artists and sculptors as opposed to designers and craftworkers.
fixative	A thin varnish sprayed onto charcoal or pastel artworks to reduce smudging.
font	A set of letters and numbers in a particular style or typeface.
foreshortening	Using the rules of perspective to make objects in a picture appear to come towards you as you look at them.
fresco	Italian for 'fresh'. Painting directly on a wall using pigments mixed with water, applied to the plaster while it is still damp so that colours are absorbed and remain fresh. The process goes back to antiquity, but was revived in the fourteenth century in southern Europe, where the climate is more suitable for frescoes than in the north.
frottage	French for 'rubbing'. Textures and patterns made by rubbing crayons or graphite on paper laid over objects or materials with raised surfaces.

Term	Description
genre	Has two meanings: **(1)** French for 'type', a category or type of artwork, as in landscape or portrait. **(2)** Paintings of everyday domestic (often peasant) life.
glaze	A shiny coating put onto ceramic work after it has been fired.
gouache	Opaque water-based paint giving strong yet flat effect. Often used in graphic design.
graffito	An original Italian technique for decorating the outside walls of houses by 'scratching' designs in the plaster.
graffiti	The plural of graffito, which has come to mean spray-painting onto walls in public places. Originally no more than simple vandalism, some graffiti artists have made the change from vandal to artist by having their skills recognised by the art world. One of the best known is the Bristol-based artist called Banksy..
ground	The primed surface of a painting.
horizon line	The horizontal line, sometimes where sky and earth appear to meet, which may be drawn across the pictorial space and corresponds to the artist's eye-level. See 'vanishing point'.
illustration	Pictures that make the meaning of something clearer and easier to understand, such as in children's storybooks, manuals and textbooks, colour magazines and brochures.
impasto	Technique where paint is applied thickly with a palette knife.
kitsch	From a German word that means 'to make cheaply'. In art and design it means poor quality, mass produced and in gaudy colours. Generally considered to be bad, but since pop art even kitsch objects have been reworked as art forms in their own right. American artist Jeff Koons is perhaps the best example.
landscape	**(1)** Pictures of the environment, either natural or built, from imagination or real-life. **(2)** Page layout that is wider than it is tall.
life drawing	Drawing the human figure from a live model (often nude).
lithography	Printmaking process based on the principle that oil and water don't mix. Invented in the late eighteenth century. A modern version, offset lithography, is used in most printing presses.
maquette	French for 'small model', a kind of 3-D sketch for a larger sculpture.
media	The materials used by artists, crafts workers and designers to make their work. The plural of 'medium': paint is a medium. When artists use different materials in their work they are said to be working in mixed media.
mobile	A sculpture made up of shapes hanging on wires that moves in the air. A type of art created by Alexander Calder around 1930.
monochrome	Tones of a single colour or a picture made in one colour only.
monoprint	Printmaking process where paper is laid on an inked surface and drawn on. Each print is a one-off.
mosaic	Decorating surfaces with small pieces of coloured glass, stone or ceramic set in cement.
mural	Painting either directly on a wall or on panels fixed to a wall.
narrative painting	Painting which tells a story.
negative space	The part of a picture or design where there is no subject. Sometimes, but not always, the background and, in a sculpture, the unfilled area of the 3-D form.

Term	Description
oil paint	Paint made by mixing pigment with oil. This has become the most common paint for artists since the early fifteenth century. It can be used thickly or thinned down and, because it takes a long time to dry, it is good for working colours into each other.
pastels	There are two types of pastels in common use. **(1)** Soft chalk pastels, which are soft and powdery and are blended together by rubbing with the finger. **(2)** Oil pastels, which are rich and greasy and are used like 'paint on a stick' by smearing and smudging colours together.
pastiche	French for 'imitation', work made in the style of another artist.
perspective	Rules by which the illusion of 3-D is created on a flat surface.
photomontage	A picture made from putting together parts of cut-out photographs.
portfolio	A large case for carrying flat works of art.
portrait	**(1)** A work of art where the main subject is a person or people; often in a setting relevant to the sitter's life, but sometimes just a head and shoulders. **(2)** Page layout that is taller than it is wide.
primary colours	The colours red, yellow and blue. In theory all other colours can be made by mixing different proportions of these three colours together.
proof	A test print made to make sure the process is working properly.
proportion	Relating the different parts of something to each other. When drawing people, for example, it is important to make sure that arms and legs are 'in proportion' to the body or torso.
relief	Type of sculpture where the shape sticks out from its background. The image may stick out in high (alto), medium (mezzo) or low (bas) relief.
replica	A one-off exact copy of an artwork made under the supervision of the original artist.
sculpture	Three-dimensional artwork created by carving, modelling or construction.
secondary colours	Colours made by mixing two primary colours together: red + yellow = orange; blue + yellow = green; red + blue = purple.
silkscreen printing	Printmaking process where ink is pushed through a stencil (fixed on a piece of silk stretched over a frame) onto a piece of paper below. Andy Warhol is perhaps most famous for using this technique in the 1960s.
sketch	Any type of drawing, painting or model made in preparation for a larger finished piece.
squaring up	A way of enlarging a small drawing on to a bigger surface. Divide both into squares and copy each square one at a time from the small drawing to the large one.
still life	An arrangement of a group of objects drawn or painted as a subject in their own right.
stipple	A process of drawing or painting where the image is made up from small dots and dashes of paint.
stretcher	Adjustable wooden frame for stretching canvas over as a support for painting.
support	The surface on which a painting is made: canvas, wood, card or paper.
three-dimensional/3-D	Art that has height, width and depth and can be seen 'in the round'. Sculpture, pottery, mobiles and clothes are 3-D.

Term	Description
transcription	Making a version of another artist's work in a new medium.
trompe l'œil	French for 'deceives the eye'. Painting that fools you into thinking it actually is the real thing.
tertiary colours	Colours made by mixing two secondary colours together.
two-dimensional/2-D	Art that has height and width. Flat pictures, such as drawings, prints, paintings and photographs, are 2-D.
vanishing point	In the rules of perspective, the point (or points) where parallel lines appear to meet on the horizon.
viewfinder	Card 'window' used as an aid when drawing to select specific parts of a scene or still life arrangement.
warm colours	Colours such as red and yellow are considered 'warm', whereas blues are thought to be 'cold'.
wash	A thin, transparent layer of diluted ink or watercolour often painted with a large flat paintbrush.
watercolour	Paint that thins with water. Traditionally colours are built up by layering thin transparent washes of paint over each other until you reach the colour you want. White is not used because the white of the paper makes colours paler.
woodcut	Printmaking process using carved blocks. The parts not cut away are the parts that print. Lino is another material used for this process.

Acknowledgements

Author acknowledgements

I would like to thank my wife, Kate; Richard Hickman; Rob Goldsworthy and the past and present students of The Park High School in King's Lynn whose work is reproduced throughout this book, specifically Lucie Auker, Daniel Bloodworth, Emma Cooper, Nicole Clarkstone, James Crown, Phillipa Escott, Sara-Jane Everitt, Victoria Harvey, Lauren Hubbard, Amy McCarthy, Josh Nurse, Dovile Paskevicuite, Kody Perez, Kirsty Reed, Emma Rowling, Emma Semple, Christie Sharpe, Stacey Softley, Simon Watson, Katie White.

This book is dedicated to Bill Read.

Image acknowledgements

Akg-images Ltd p56 (*I love you with my Ford*, 1961, oil on canvas, 210 x 237,5 cm, James Rosenquist, © James Rosenquist// DACS, London/VAGA, New York 2009), p54 (Frida Kahlo/*Self-Portrait*/1930. © 2009, Banco de México, Diego Rivera & Frida Kahlo Museums Trusts, Mexico D.F./DACS); The Art Archive p39 (Awa Province Naruto rapids/Victoria and Albert Museum London/Sally Chappell); The Bridgeman Art Library/www.bridgemanart.co.uk p28 (Tso Elephant Mask, Cameroon Grasslands, African/Private Collection, Heini Schneebeli), p29 (Ostrakon, Egyptian, 19th Dynasty (c.1297–1185 BC)/ Egyptian Museum, Turin, Italy, Alinari), p30 (Yoruba Door Carving, wood, Nigerian/Private Collection, Heini Schneebeli), p32 (Mayan vessel, Nebaj, Alta Verapaz, Guatemala, AD700–800/British Museum, London, UK), p34 (*Alex*, 1991, Close, Chuck (b.1940)/Cecil Higgins Art Gallery, Bedford, Bedfordshire, UK/© Chuck Close, courtesy PaceWildenstein, New York), p35 (*Detroit Industry*, north wall, 1933, fresco (detail), Rivera, Diego (1886–1957)/© 2009, Banco de México, Diego Rivera & Frida Kahlo Museums Trusts, Mexico DF, DACS), p36 (Enamelled vase,19th century, Japanese School/© Leeds Museums and Art Galleries (Temple Newsam House) UK), (Samurai Warrior's Armour, Japanese School/Tower of London, London, UK), p38 (*Blossoms*, one of twelve leaves inscribed with a poem from an *Album of Fruit and Flowers*, ink and colour on paper, Chen Hongshou (1768-1821)/Private Collection, Christie's Images), p40 (Rock art, pig nosed turtle, c.1960s (photo) Kakaku National Park, Australia), p41 (*The Kiss*, 1907 (stone), Brancusi, Constantin © ADAGP, Paris and DACS, London 2009), p44 (Proportions of the human figure, c.1492 (*Vitruvian Man*), pen & ink on paper, Vinci, Leonardo da (1452–1519)/Galleria dell' Accademia, Venice, Italy), p45 (*The Cherry Picker*, oil on canvas, Morisot, Berthe (1841–95)/Musee Marmottan, Paris, France, Giraudon), p47 (*The Pine Tree at St. Tropez*, 1909, oil on canvas, Signac, Paul (1863-1935)/Pushkin Museum, Moscow, Russia), p48 (Floral wallpaper design, Morris, William (1834–96)/Private Collection, The Stapleton Collection), p49 (*The "Fighting Temeraire" Tugged to her Last Berth to be Broken up*, before 1839, Turner, Joseph Mallord William (1775–1851)/ National Gallery, London, UK), p50 (*"Just what is it that makes today's homes so different, so appealing?"*, 1959, collage, Hamilton, Richard (b.1922)/Kunsthalle, Tubingen, Germany/© Richard Hamilton 2009. All Rights Reserved, DACS 2009), p53 (*Pineapple with Insects*, engraved by J. Mulder, plate 1 from '*The Metamorphosis of the Insects of Surinam*', c.1699–1701, hand-coloured engraving, Merian, Maria Sibylla Graff (1647–1717) (after)/Natural History Museum, London, UK), p 53 (Leather chair, with black lacquered frame, by Eileen Gray (1879–1976), c.1930/Private Collection), p54 (*Untitled* (Self-Portrait of Marilyn Monroe), 1982, ektachrome photograph, Sherman, Cindy (b.1954)/© Museum of Fine Arts, Houston, Texas, USA/© Courtesy of the Artist and Metro Pictures), p56 (Andy Warhol – 25 Coloured Marilyns Twenty Marilyns, 1962 (silk screen), Warhol, Andy (1930–87) © The Andy Warhol Foundation for the Visual Arts/Artists Rights Society (ARS), New York and DACS, London 2009), p59 (*George and the Dragon*, 1984, plastic, wood and aluminium, Cragg, Tony (b.1949)/Arts Council Collection, Hayward Gallery, London, UK/ Courtesy the artist and Lisson Gallery); Corbis p39 (Bollywood poster/ Sandro Vannini); eBoy p 46 (*PCHOME*, 1998–2005 eBoy (Steffen Sauerteig, Svend Smital, Peter Stemmler, Kai Vermehr) www.eboy.com Courtesy of artist); Getty Images p35 (Donna Karan fashion show/Scott Gries); Lonely Planet Images p45 (Chimneys, Antonio Gaudi/Martin Hughes); Shutterstock – all used under licence from Shutterstock.com p32 (© Ieva Geneviciene, 2009), p33 (© Gary Yim, 2009), p37 (© Jennifer Stone, 2009), p40 (© Afaizal, 2009), p42 (© Jenny Solomon, 2009), p43 (© Ruth Black, 2009), p48 (© Phillip Minnis, 2009); Werner Forman Archive p30 (Kuba Textile, Congo, Equatorial Africa, 20th century/Anspach Collection, New York); p31 (*Royal Tide IV*, 1959/60, found object construction spray painted, Louise Nevelson/© ARS, NY and DACS, London 2009); p51 (*Bone China Textured Veil bowl*, 12cm h. by Sasha Wardell/ photo Mark Lawrence. Courtesy of artist); p55 (*Round the World*, 1958/9, oil on canvas, Sam Francis © Sam L. Francis Foundation/DACS, London 2009); p57 (*Spiral Jetty*, 1970, Robert Smithson/© Estate of Robert Smithson DACS, London/ VAGA, New York 2009); p58 (*Landscape No. 2*, 1964, Tom Wesselmann/© Estate of Tom Wesselmann/DACS, London/VAGA, NY, 2009).